The Character
of Adoption

by the same author

SECRETARY

The Character of Adoption

Mary Kathleen Benet

JONATHAN CAPE
THIRTY BEDFORD SQUARE LONDON

FIRST PUBLISHED 1976
© 1976 BY MARY KATHLEEN BENET

JONATHAN CAPE LTD, 30 BEDFORD SQUARE, LONDON WCI

ISBN 0 224 01199 5

SET IN 11 PT BASKERVILLE I PT LEADED
PRINTED IN GREAT BRITAIN BY
COX & WYMAN LTD,
LONDON, FAKENHAM AND READING

For Arthur and Giulietta

Contents

Preface

What terminology to use in a book about adoption is as political a question as adoption itself. Should the term 'natural mother' be used, with its implication that adopters are unnatural? What about 'biological parents'—are adopters made of plastic? 'First parents' has an uneasy analogy with 'first marriage'.

Should a social worker be referred to as 'she', when the term has about a 90 per cent chance of being the correct one? The English language may allow us to use 'he' to mean 'he or she' when referring to the adopted child; but will the women's movement allow us to do so? Should 'black' be capitalized, even if 'white' is not?

In the interests of clarity, I have generally followed the usage of other writers on the subject—without, I hope, treading on too many toes.

I would like to thank Jane Rowe of the A.B.A.A.; Arlene Nash of ARENA and the library staff of the C.W.L.A.; Ursula Gallagher of the United States Children's Bureau; Tim Morris of the D.H.S.S.; and all the social workers and adoptive families who so willingly gave their time to be interviewed. John Wolfers read drafts and elicited ideas in Socratic fashion; my husband, Julian Hale, gave unfailing support and encouragement as well as skilled editing.

1 Introduction

The decision to adopt a child is a plunge into the unknown. Even the least complicated adoption brings the participants face to face with some very basic—and perhaps unexpected—feelings: attitudes towards kinship and inheritance, the relative importance of the family and the outside world, sexual morality, self-interest and altruism are all called into question.

In the West today, adoption is accepted as the neat and sensible solution to the problems of two groups of people: childless couples and children without families. It is easy for people to begin by assuming that their own attitudes and practices are the norm—the natural, commonsensical way to behave. But the fact is that adoption has taken utterly different forms throughout history and around the world—at some times all but disappearing, at others becoming almost universal. And our muddled, ambivalent attitudes are the result of an uneasy mingling of different traditions.

In many ways, we are still unsure whether children can be fully transplanted into another family, or whether the ties of blood will prove ineradicable. Adoption is a recent addition to the legal codes of the English-speaking countries, and it has made its way against a belief in the absolute primacy of the biological link between parents and children. In English common law, parental rights and duties were traditionally inalienable—the first Adoption Act was passed only in 1926.

Led by the United States, the Western countries have passed ever more comprehensive adoption laws, severing the child's links with his original family and giving him equal status with the biological children of his new parents. Adoption has grown in popularity since the Second World War, and most people now believe that it has shown itself to be a viable institution.

Recent studies indicate that adopted children do at least as well in life as children raised by their own families, and far better than children raised by a single mother.

More recent doubts about adoption stem from today's controversies over inequality, imperialism, and the nature of the family itself. These are political questions. They are not about the ability of an adoptive family to provide enough security and love for a growing child. They are about the matter of who adopts whom. Adoption has usually meant the transfer of a child from one social class to another slightly higher one. Today, as always, adopters tend to be richer than the natural parents of the children they adopt. They may also be members of a racial majority, adopting children of a minority; or citizens of a rich country, adopting children from a poor one.

Adopters themselves feel bad about this. Many take the political dimension of adoption very personally, and have trouble justifying it to themselves or to their adopted children. They cannot bear to think about the situation of the natural mother, or to explain it to the child. Others seek in individual circumstances an escape from wider questions. They may point to the youth of the natural mother, or to her emotional problems, as evidence that their particular adoption was not associated with inequality or social injustice.

Most advice on the subject gives little help to adopters as they work their way through this dilemma. Indeed, the political dimension is usually ignored. Practical tips are given about agencies, telling the child of his adoption, identity crises, and inheritance—but the moral questions that torment so many adopters often shrink to a discussion of the charitable aspect of adoption. It used to be that the child himself was spoken of as fortunate in being rescued by a kind family; now the family itself is considered fortunate to be allowed to adopt a child in conditions of scarcity.

To talk about adoption on any but a strictly personal level, it is necessary to assemble information from many sources. The study of adoption rests on a borderline between sociology and psychology: patterns of family life and social mobility are clearly relevant, as are theories about the development of the human psyche. What aspects of the personality are formed by membership of a particular social group? How can one measure individual reactions, genetically programmed or not, to individual experience? Adoption raises these questions and can also help to answer them. Thus the study of adoption has wide relevance to other fields, as well as to future adoption practice. In many ways, psychological and sociological information carries implications for practice. The emotional needs of children, and the mechanisms by which a social group survives or disintegrates, can be studied with a view to making the system work better. But even when we have assembled both these types of information, we are not yet in a position to answer questions about the moral and political dimensions of adoption.

We can learn from comparing the practice of adoption in different times and places that the moral views of every society have influenced its practice of adoption much more heavily than have pragmatic considerations. Inescapably, this is so. To a society based on religion, the importance of choosing adopters who practise that religion obviously takes precedence. In an aristocratic society, opportunity for a child is often defined as access to the ruling group. Democrats feel adoption should be regulated with some notion of equal opportunity.

In today's secular, pluralistic societies, what is right is usually more or less defined as what works best, especially when it comes to the care of children. But even in the West, adoption practice is influenced by broad notions of what sort of society we want to have. Opponents of sexual licence, for example, have sometimes been hostile to adoption on the grounds that it allows unmarried mothers to 'get away with it'. More recently, adoption has been attacked as a rich people's charter against minority groups. Such examples of the political dimension of adoption thinking can be multiplied many times over.

Adopters have often been unwilling, even afraid, to confront adoption as a political question. They say, 'I believe in individual solutions,' or 'At least one child will have a loving family and enough to eat.' In a sense, they are quite right: adoption has never been a wholesale operation, and no one would suggest that it can even begin to solve the enormous problems of poverty and homelessness facing the world today.

But adopters need not fear that a look at adoption as a political phenomenon will cast them as the villains of the piece.

13

To say that the biological parents of adopted children are to some degree victims of the social system is not the same as saying that adoption should stop. On the contrary, as we shall see, the most egalitarian and efficient societies, in terms of providing for all their children, have always practised adoption on a far wider scale than any of the countries of the industrial West have yet dreamt of.

It is worth studying the countries where adoption is (or has been) a strong tradition, because they differ in some fundamental ways from the Western nations that have passed modern adoption laws. Typically, widespread adoption has been part of a strong extended family system of a type that the industrial revolution long since destroyed in the West. It is true that adoption is part of what remains of our own family system: even today in England and the United States, half of all adoptions are between relatives. And adoption as such has always been known in Western countries, even during the periods when no adoption laws were on the books. But what we usually mean by the simple, unqualified word 'adoption' today is the adoption of a non-related child, whose parents are unknown to us, through an agency or some other go-between.

Other societies, too, have practised non-relative adoption: in ancient Rome and traditional Japan, it was a means of allying oneself, or at least one's child, with a ruling family. But in China and India, relatives were preferred adoptees when it came to selecting an heir for a sonless family. In many primitive societies, informal adoption or fostering was regularly practised as a means of cementing the social ties among kin.

What is missing from all these examples is the characteristically Western notion that the primary reason for adoption is to rescue a child separated from his natural family. Although most other forms of adoption could be extended to cover such cases, they were very far from being the norm. The Western ideal is to completely sever the links between the adoptee and his original family, and for natural parents and adopters to remain unknown to each other. This desire for secrecy would seem bizarre to most other practitioners of adoption—to the ancients, the Asians, and the primitives, adoption was more often than not a quite deliberate transaction between two sets of parents.

14

There is one very obvious reason for the West's distinctive approach to adoption. In the absence of a strong historical tradition of adoption, laws were framed to meet a new situation: the break-up of the extended family under the impact of industrialization and urbanization. Dr John Bowlby, the major theorist of children's need for a permanent attachment figure, says:

> It is probably only in communities in which the greater family group has ceased to exist that the problem of deprived children is found on a serious scale ... Not only does such a broken-up community provide no substitutes should a mother or father be temporarily or permanently incapacitated but, by putting this great load on parents, it may destroy a family which in better circumstances could hold together.[1]

This emphasis on the nuclear family means that the few remaining ties—those between husband and wife, parents and children—are closer and more intense than ever before. The tribe member can surrender his children with comparative equanimity, knowing that the separation is not complete and that he in turn will receive other children to foster. But to the modern parent, relinquishing a child for adoption deprives him of one of his only human contacts. Thus the only children who are given up for adoption are those whose own parents are really unable to keep them—either because of the opprobrium attached to unmarried parenthood or because of poverty, extreme youth and other practical handicaps.

There are many options society can explore in caring for its unwanted children, and Western countries have used several of them. But institutions have, by and large, not met the emotional needs of the children; and fostering provides neither the permanence required by the children nor the legal security desired by their substitute parents. Western law and practice has been gradually moving in the direction of ever more secure and complete transfer of parental roles—and this means that adoption has an increasing edge over the other methods. It appeals both to the child-care workers, interested in the well-being of their charges, and to the legislators, interested in saving money, as the Director of the National Children's Bureau in England makes clear in saying that 'adoption provides the most satisfactory form of permanent care—and incidentally the cheapest—yet devised by Western society for socially deprived children whose own parents cannot undertake it.'[2]

The post-war increase in the popularity of adoption came about because it solved a particular social problem: the rise in white middle-class illegitimacy during the 'permissive society' of the 1950s and 1960s. Society has now caught up with its own permissiveness, and abortion and contraception are the order of the day. Interest in adoption, however, has not abated, especially since (as some observers believe) the stresses of over-populated urban life may be increasing the rate of infertility. Thus the dwindling supply of adoptable babies has created a crisis, a hunt for other sources that has led to a searching examination of the way children everywhere are presently being cared for. Children in institutions, battered babies, war orphans—none of these are new, but their plight seems particularly intolerable now that there are so many people being frustrated in their desire to adopt.

Today's adoptive parents are reacting to the shortage of perfect white infants by extending adoption to new groups of children. Childless couples are no longer virtually the only adopters, and they are no longer necessarily looking for the child who might have been born to them. A recent meeting of the adoptive parents' groups in the United States made the change quite clear:

> adoptive families have cast aside the conventional notion of blood ties. This fact is most visible when families do not attempt to 'match' their superficial physical characteristics, but instead settle for a less naive relationship. Most of us at 4th N.A.C.A.C. have entered into a 'complex' adoptive relationship. Complex adoption ignores conventional distinctions and founds kinship on reciprocal need, caring, and affinity ... The North American experiment with complex adoption, virtually unique in world history, has matured to the point of being a proven phenomenon.[3]

Complex adoption might even be said to be the currently preferred method of creating a family, as the Director of the C.W.L.A. suggested at the same conference.

> Because of this deep concern for our country's and other countries' children, a Presbyterian preacher on the west coast said in a sermon that it was immoral to bear children of your own if there were children waiting for a family. This is one of the reasons for the enormous surge in interest in adoption in the United States ... a major advance in the discussion of morality.[4]

Even in the United States, where adoption was accepted more readily than in Europe with its hereditary notions of status, it is none the less viewed as second-best, as something that is not 'supposed' to happen. It is, in most people's minds, an indication that the child's original parents failed to care for him, and that his adoptive parents failed to have their own children.

However, the nuclear family itself is under increasing attack as a source of neurosis and stress, and a wider view of the possibilities of adoption is very much part of the current debate about the role of the family. Challengers of the small-family orthodoxy know that there have been, and still are, many societies where adoption is the *preferred* way to raise children. All the ethnic groups peripheral to American society — blacks, Indians, Eskimos, Polynesians — have practised kinship fostering or outright adoption to a much greater extent than has the Wasp majority. Adoption in these groups is a means of strengthening the extended family, and society as a whole, by weakening the exclusive bond between parents and children. Co-operation and good will are promoted by dividing up parental functions, and the tensions and ambivalence of the nuclear family are relieved.

In spite of the efforts of American youth to investigate alternative life styles, there is little hope that tribal or extended-family systems can be revived on a large scale in our own day. And as long as they exist only on a small and marginal scale, they will not be sufficiently permanent to raise children. But widespread interest in these methods indicates that people want to know how a fluid, open and heterogeneous society can be made as humane and responsive to the needs of its members as the closed societies of primitive man once were.

The sharing of parental roles is one concept that modern man has learned from tribal man without being able to apply it in his own life. The exclusive nature of adoption has been strengthened during this century, and it is only quite recently that people have begun asking whether this is in fact a good thing. It was necessary to go through a phase of insistence on the completeness of adoption, to make sure that it was fully accepted. But now that there are few doubters of the efficacy of adoption, there has been a loosening-up of the secrecy that used to surround the subject. Adoptive children have become franker in their desire for information about their origins, and adoptive parents are increasingly relaxed about accepting this curiosity as normal. Concepts like legal guardianship and long-term fostering, which have long been in disrepute, are being re-examined. The adoption of older children, which cannot be successful if it is based on attempts to bury the past, is being handled in increasingly skilful ways.

The customs of other societies are thus a source of ideas that modern adoption workers, and parents themselves, are interested in from the point of view of their own practice. There are, however, two other kinds of information that they will find necessary before they can implement these ideas.

The first is the history of adoption in the West itself—which is to a large extent a history of its victory over the many obstacles placed in its path. The objections to adoption that have been lodged in the past still influence practice today, and mistrust of the motives of the parties concerned is the agencies' chief inheritance from the days when adopters were thought to be interested in exploiting the children, and relinquishing mothers thought to be trying to get out of their own responsibilities. The punitive attitude to poverty, which the English Poor Laws codified and sent around the world, is another aspect of this inheritance, and has been very hard to eradicate in the practice of adoption. The agencies themselves, with their overlapping and conflicting areas of jurisdiction, are relics of the division of poor relief and welfare work among the Church, the secular authorities, and private charities.

The other thing adopters need to know in order to change

their methods for the better is how well adoption actually works today. What effect does it have on the participants? How does it compare with other methods of raising children?

It is difficult to evaluate the success of any family in measurable terms. Studies of the outcome of adoptions therefore find it hard to agree on the criteria of success. One uses the children's eventual capacity for adult relationships, or their adult earning power. Another bases its judgments on how members of the family describe its functioning. The proportion of adopted children treated in psychiatric clinics is another index.

By any set of criteria, however, it appears that adoptive families compare well to ordinary ones. The National Child Development Study, in England, is perhaps the most comprehensive experiment to date. It followed the progress of all the children born in one week of 1958, and thus was able to compare the adopted children with a cross-section of their age-mates. The adopted children not only were doing better, at the age of 7, than the children who stayed with their unmarried mothers — they were also doing better than the cohort as a whole. They were taller than the average, and

> in all the aspects of ability and attainment which were examined, they did either as well as, or even better than, all the other children in the cohort.
>
> Overall, the adopted did markedly better than the other cohort children in respect of general knowledge and oral ability, and as well as them in their level of creativity.[5]

The hypothesis of the researchers is that these striking results show that the selection process adoptive parents go through, and their deliberate desire for children, more than offset any stressful and unsettling experiences the children may have had as a result of being adopted.

Other studies have indicated that adoptive families have unique strengths and weaknesses, not all of which operate to the child's advantage. Many researchers feel that the adopted child, no matter how secure, is bound to suffer from 'genealogical bewilderment': that is, he may feel a lingering sense of rejection stemming from his separation from his biological parents. Adoptees themselves have often confirmed this, although much depends on how they are taught to view their adoption. The psychologist Ner Littner has spoken of the 'Achilles Heel' of the adopted child—the fear of another traumatic separation and the consequent unwillingness to make deep emotional commitments. Dr Winnicott, the famous British child psychiatrist who treated many adopted children, suggested that their sexual confusion at adolescence might be the consequence of an incomplete incest taboo in the adoptive family.

On the other hand, adopted children know they are wanted. They are surrounded by so much anxious care that the adopted child's personality is likely to resemble that of the only child: he becomes a worrier and a high achiever. This may be why, although adopted children seem more neurotic than the average on clinical tests in childhood, their performance as adults seems surprisingly unaffected by their neurosis. The ordinary measurements do not apply to them, because they are having a different experience of life.

Research on adoption, which is being carried out on an increasing scale especially in the United States, has obvious implications for practice. Adopters—and the social workers who place the children—want to know what sort of parent copes best with adoption; how and when the child should be told of his status; what sorts of behaviour to expect and how to deal with them.

Beyond this, adopters want to know how to answer what is probably the most serious political question facing them today. The morality of adoption itself has been called into question by many of the groups who are currently supplying the greatest numbers of adoptable children. American blacks and the governments of many poor countries have objected to the movement for trans-racial and international adoption, which they see as compounding the injustices already visited upon them by the capitalist metropolis. In a system of gross economic inequality, they say, is it right that the weaker groups should be systematically deprived first of their ability to make a living, and then of the children they are unable to support?

On the other hand, the adopters reply, must the welfare and the very lives of children be imperilled while universal solutions to poverty are sought?

This is the vexed moral question facing adoption today. And while there is no clear answer to it, adopters are increasingly certain that the success of their families vindicates their stance. For adopters have often been well ahead of governments and social agencies in their recognition of the needs of children and their response to those needs. They have pressed for the placement of children labelled 'hard-to-place' by the agencies; they have helped to recruit minority-group adopters; they have helped to cut through outmoded selection criteria.

Adoptive parents do not have to shoulder the blame for family break-up and the relinquishment of children. Rather, they can help to place the blame where it belongs: on a social system that impoverishes and punishes certain groups of people. Armed with the facts about adoption, they can help to change that system and to make adoption part of a more humane and realistic set of alternatives for children and their families.

39681

2 The Extended Family

'...there seems to be an intrinsic wisdom, or at any rate an unconscious planfulness, in the seemingly arbitrary varieties of cultural conditioning: in fact, homogeneous cultures provide certain balances in later life for the very desires, fears, and rages which they provoked in childhood.'

Erik Erikson, *Childhood and Society*

Adoption is as old as human society itself. Tradition has it that our culture was begun by foundlings: Romulus and Remus suckled by the wolf, and Moses rescued from the bulrushes by Pharaoh's daughter. This is part of the general propensity of civilizations to invent myths about their supernatural origin — their founders must be seen as belonging unequivocally to the new order rather than to the old, and one way to achieve this discontinuity is to make a mystery of their parentage and the circumstances of their birth.

So it is that stories involving adoption play a part in many religions and myths of group origin, whether or not the group itself subsequently practises it: this will be determined by such factors as the system of land-holding and inheritance, the ratio of population to land, and the degree of social stratification.

Some use of adoption has been part of the 'unconscious planfulness' of most homogeneous societies. The extent of its use has typically found a balance with other mechanisms for providing children with families and vice versa. Classical Eurasian societies — in Rome, China and India — practised adoption, as did the tribal societies of, for example, tropical Africa and Oceania. Since these two groups of societies have many things in common, there are, not surprisingly, some similarities in their use of adoption. In both, members of the extended family were the preferred adoptees, and adoption was a transaction between the two sets of parents. To contrast their systems in other respects, and to compare each with adoption in the West, tells us much about the nature of the institution itself. In particular, it corrects the impression prevailing in the West that the 'blood tie' has historical precedence over forms of social kinship, and that it takes a complex modern society to invent adoption.

There are many reasons why adoption was important as far back as we can see in human history. Survival, especially that of children, was uncertain. To ensure the continuity of the group, it was necessary to have flexible arrangements for incorporating new members and providing substitute parents. For a ruling group to keep power, it had to attach to itself enough talented members of the next generation.

From the very earliest times a distinction was made between social and physical paternity—and the former was usually the more important. Social paternity has typically been established by the mother's marriage. The Romans said *pater est quem nuptiae demonstrant*; the early English, "whoso boleth my kyne, ewere calf is mine". It was this distinction that made adoption possible. It was obviously impossible to change physical paternity, but, in social terms, parental rights were theoretically transferable. However, adoption raised some unique problems, which were quickly recognized and which have persisted to this day.

The oldest written set of laws is the Babylonian code of Hammurabi, which contains a long, sophisticated section on adoption. It deals with some of the risks inherent in every adoption: that the adoptive parents will treat the child differently from a natural child; that the child will suffer from a change of caretaker; and that the adopted child and family will be unsuited to each other.

Babylonian adoption only remained valid as long as the adopter treated the child in every way as his own; if the child 'persisted in searching for its father and its mother', it was returned to the natural parents. The issue of 'maternal deprivation' was already known and faced.

The only adopted child whose ingratitude was severely

punished was the one adopted by a courtier, who was prevented by law (and sometimes by castration) from begetting his own children. This kind of adoption was a signal honour, and involved a great leap in social status for the child.

> The [adopted] son of a chamberlain or the [adopted] son of an epicene shall not be [re]claimed ... If the [adopted] son of an epicene states to the father who has brought him up or the mother who has brought him up 'Thou art not my father' [or] 'Thou art not my mother', they shall cut out his tongue.[1]

Two other special cases are included by Hammurabi under the heading of adoption: apprenticeship and wet-nursing. Boys were adopted by free craftsmen to learn and inherit the trade, but the adoption was invalid if the craftsman did not teach his lore. Any adopter was likely to have need of a wet-nurse, who would be in charge of the child for two or three years. There were strict rules relating to her conduct, and there were fierce penalties if a child died while in her care.

What were the Babylonians' reasons for adopting? We have seen that the craftsman and the courtier had special reasons, but in ordinary cases:

> In Babylonia the main object of adoption was originally to acquire a son to perpetuate the family and to perform the religious rites due to the adopter after his death; but purely secular reasons, such as the continuation of his business or his maintenance in old age, also played their part in this institution. The Attic rule that a man could adopt a son only if he had none was not strictly observed in Babylonia, although it seems to have been usual ... [2]

These 'secular reasons' still operate today, in spite of claims that adoption is now practised chiefly in the interests of the child.

In the ancient world adoption was only one of many ways of obtaining heirs. Solutions needed to be found for both male and female infertility, and although many of the ancient methods — polygamy, legitimation — are still in use today, there is one way of obtaining legal descendants that has completely died out. This is the levirate, under which a man inherited his brother's widow and 'raised up' children to the dead man.

> The custom of the levirate was obviously derived or continued from the desire common to all ancient peoples to ensure the continuance of the family and thereby of the ancestral property and the ancestral cult. The Babylonians and the Assyrians attained this end by polygamy, by the legitimation of the children of slave-wives and concubines, by the begetting of children on a wife's maid, and by adoption.[3]

Which of these methods were used had obvious relation to the reasons behind the desire for children. The demands of religion and inheritance could be satisfied by methods like the levirate, but this was only of interest to a landed proprietor: the craftsman, for example, cannot pass on his skill to a son born after his death.

The economic organization of society is one of the major determinants of the method chosen to obtain heirs. In the ancient Middle East, two divergent trends can be discerned.

The Babylonians, farming the great Tigris–Euphrates valley, inherited and passed on tracts of land associated with ancestor cults. In this way they resemble the peoples of China and India. The assumption of a name and a cult went with the inheritance of land, whether the line was one of blood or of adoption. It was a form of contractual agreement—and indeed a contract was drawn up for every Babylonian adoption, setting out the terms of inheritance and the obligations of both parties.

The other distinctive social system was that of the nomadic desert tribes. The Israelites were the earliest people to show the shift to this kind of economy, and thus to a new attitude towards the ancient ways of obtaining heirs. Traditionally, they practised the levirate, of which there are many examples in the Old Testament. The legitimation of the children of concubines and maids was also known, but there is a great deal of doubt about adoption. It is often asserted that there are examples of adoption in the Bible, but the *Encyclopedia Judaica* disagrees: 'The evidence for adoption in the Bible is so equivocal that some have denied it was practised in the biblical period ... Adoption is not known as a legal institution in Jewish law.'[4]

The turning point between the old ways and the new may well have come in the time of Abraham. The Biblical story mythologizes what was probably an historical sequence: Abraham considers adopting an heir in the ancient manner, but God makes it possible for Abraham and Sarah, now well past childbearing age, to have Isaac, an heir of the blood. The alternatives of adoption and the legitimation of a servant's child are considered and rejected, and it is the covenant with God — in other words, a new social and religious orientation — that allows them to be abandoned.

This coincides with God's prediction that the descendants of Abraham will wander for generations until they inherit the land that is rightfully theirs. The change in inheritance patterns, and the rejection of adoption, seem to have gone with a change to a nomadic way of life.

As a result of this change, the old ancestor cults were abandoned, and in some cases consciously suppressed.

> both [the levirate] and the other methods of perpetuating the family were discouraged by the religious reformers of the nation as these disapproved of anything tending to the worship of ancestors.[5]

The tearing down of idols that continues into the New Testament is a replacement of settled fertility cults by the new nomadic God. The other famous adoption in the Old Testament, that of Moses, only proves that the Egyptians — another settled agricultural people — knew of adoption, but not necessarily that the Israelites did. And the fact that Moses returned to his own people to lead them against the Egyptians is enough to make any potential adopter think twice.

From the nomadic peoples of the Middle East came the three great transcendent religions — Judaism, Christianity, and Islam. In many ways, their approach to adoption is similar and reflects their common origins. In these religions, man's relationship with God is that of son to father — it is consciously stated in some Biblical commentaries that the relationship of the Chosen People to God is that of an adopted child to its new parent.

Part of the old ideology survives—the obligations felt by the adoptee are a return for the land conferred upon him. The Christian mythology goes even further in the religious creation of a fictive family: nuns are the brides of Christ, the Mother Church complements God the Father, and the Holy Trinity parallels the nuclear family. In Medieval times, the substitution of the Church for the family, in the monastic orders for example, became even more apparent.

One of the salient characteristics of the transcendent desert God is omniscience—and the notion that God will not be fooled by adoption or any other fiction is one argument against it. The Koran says,

> Allah has never put two hearts within one man's body. He does not regard the wives whom you divorce as your mothers, nor your adopted sons as your own sons. These are mere words which you utter with your mouths: but Allah declares the truth and guides to the right path. Name your adopted sons after their fathers; that is more just in the sight of Allah. If you do not know their fathers, regard them as your brothers in the faith and as your wards. Your unintentional mistakes shall be forgiven, but not your deliberate errors.
>
> xxxiii, 4–6

This passage shows that Islamic law, like that of most modern Muslim countries, allowed the rescue of abandoned children without permitting adoption.

Islam is the religion that has remained most strongly opposed to adoption—modern Israel has an adoption law, as do most Christian countries. One of the first Muslim states to pass such a law, Tunisia, did so mainly to prevent non-Muslims from adopting Tunisian children out of the country and the faith— more as a defensive than a prescriptive measure. In part, this is because Islam also continued a tradition of polygamy and easy divorce; in all societies, adoption is in widespread use where alternatives to it are few, and vice versa.

The patriarchal nature of Islam also militates against adoption. A man can legitimate his own child simply by recognizing it; marriage with the mother is not strictly necessary. A

27

man can also recognize any child of his wife, even if it is the product of adultery. The male need for an heir is thus catered for, and the fact that there is no recourse for an infertile woman does not matter in such a male-dominated society. Infertility is never attributed to the male: it is believed that somewhere there is a woman by whom he can have children.

In all of these religions, the faith is more important than the family. Adoption in the West has grown only as religious belief has declined—contrary to the view that adoption is an outgrowth of 'Christian charity'.

Jewishness is passed on through the mother—that is, the child of a Jewish mother is Jewish, regardless of the religion of the father, but the reverse is not true. Orthodox marriage and other church rituals are not permitted to non-Jews, and so adoption creates special problems, even today.

> It is essential that Jewish adoptive parents should be advised before adopting a child to consult the Beth Din [Jewish Ecclesiastical Court] so as to make sure that the child to be adopted is Jewish. The Beth Din keeps a register of adopted children, so that when the question of marriage arises the existence of such registration will prevent any difficulties. The fact that a child has been brought up in a Jewish home does not by itself constitute Jewishness in the ecclesiastical meaning of the word.[6]

There have, in the West, been very few Jewish children available for adoption, but many Jews who wanted to adopt; most of these have ceased to be Orthodox, so that the issue is no longer a live one. The religion has not changed, it has simply been by-passed.

Similarly, Christian countries have continued to use the adoption laws inherited from a variety of other sources, and the Church has accommodated itself more or less to these. It has imposed a few restrictions about allowing children to be adopted by those of another religion, and about the baptism of adopted children.

Catholics have, by and large, opposed adoption more often than they have promoted it. Because of the Church's opposition to birth control, there have often been many Catholic babies available for adoption and few Catholics who wanted to add to their own large families by this means. None the less, the Church has preferred to keep the children in Catholic institutions rather than to allow adoption by non-Catholics. Social workers say that if a child has a secure family, he doesn't need much else, and without that, it doesn't matter what else he has. Catholics seem to attach the same importance to the faith; the two notions continue to coexist uneasily. Recruitment to the Church has always been the prevailing idea behind the varying Catholic attitudes to adoption; it was approved when it could be turned to the Church's advantage.

The early Church, with its history of asceticism and its suspicion of the family, is the source of much of this thinking. The Christians, as an embattled minority, were more interested in conversion and recruitment than in founding personal dynasties; the radical separation between the Church and the societies around it, the disregard of material property (natural enough in a group that had very little), the belief in immortality —all worked against the establishment of mechanisms of personal continuity like adoption.

The Christian Church grew up in the old-established society of the Roman Empire. This affected its development, and gave it a background that was not part of the original desert heritage. The laws and customs of Rome were directly descended from the Babylonians and the Greeks, and the structure of their society was, at least in the early days, quite similar.

Roman law developed over many centuries, but it seems that adoption was always part of it. In Rome, too, there was a tradition of ancestor cults, and tending the cult was the adoptee's return for the land he inherited. Rich Romans were anxious to trace their lineage from the founders and heroes of the nation, and Gibbon explains that this was part of the mechanism by which successful adventurers tried to consolidate their positions.

> The vanity of the rich who desired to be noble was gratified by these lofty pretensions. Encouraged by the applause of their parasites, they easily imposed on the credulity of the vulgar, and were countenanced in some measure by the custom of adopting the name of their patron, which had

always prevailed among the freedmen and clients of illustrious families.[7]

Patricians, even emperors, adopted successors to cut out possible claimants of which they disapproved; a successful general, for example, could be adopted by a rich family as a reward for valour.

The problem faced by Roman adoption law was reconciliation with the total power of the *paterfamilias*. How could a person be adopted if he was under the sway of such power, which was inalienable and irrevocable? A complicated two-tier system, which is still to be seen in the adoption laws of the Mediterranean countries, was finally worked out.

By the time of Justinian, this system was well-established. Full adoption, *adrogatio*, was only possible for a person who was himself *sui iuris*—that is, a member of no family but his own. Even an adult could be *alieni iuris*, a subordinate member of a family, if his father were still alive; equally, a child whose father had died was *sui iuris*.

If such a full adoption took place, the adoptee and all his descendants belonged to the new family. His previous cult was destroyed, and he worshipped his new ancestors.

> *Adrogatio* destroyed a family and thus was allowed only to save another, i.e. to provide a *heres* ... It was allowed only as a last resort, to save a family, and no one might adrogate more than one, or any, if he had a child already. He must be 60 or from some cause unlikely to have children.[8]

A minor could not be adrogated, because a minor *sui iuris* had *tutores*, or guardians, who had to be prevented from abusing their power by adopting their ward and appropriating his wealth.

Adoptio, or simple adoption, on the other hand, was permissible even to one who had heirs, and the adoptee in such a case could be *alieni iuris*. However, this left the problem of breaking the power of the *paterfamilias* over the person to be adopted. This power, or *potestas*, had to be renounced three times before the child was free for adoption.

The elaborate form is derived from a rule of the XII Tables (aimed at checking the cruelty and avarice of some fathers), which provided that if a father sold a son three times the son should be free from *potestas*. The *potestas* being in principle indestructible, the rule was seized on as a means of ending it at will. The transaction had two parts, a preliminary sale or sales to destroy the *potestas*, and the act of adoption, the claim and declaration in court.[9]

This is particularly interesting in comparison with English law, which also faced (and for several centuries failed to solve) the problem of inalienable parental status that was one of the major obstacles to adoption legislation. The solution found by the Romans, that of making the termination of rights a separate operation from the adoption itself, has become part of modern Western thinking.

Adoptio minus plena, as simple adoption was called by Justinian, could be done for several reasons. A father might sell his child, if he had more than he could support; and a parent whose own children were unsatisfactory to him could cut them out by adopting. Rich families tended to accumulate dependents in this way, and poor families attempted to improve their children's status by having them adopted upwards. Adoption was also used to legitimate a man's children by a concubine, although this practice gradually died out, with concubinage itself, in the Christian Empire.

Roman law is often contrasted with modern law because of its insistence that full adoption was only permissible to provide an heir for the childless. But, as we have seen, this was only true of adrogation—ordinary adoption could take place for any number of other reasons—and some of the provisions of Roman adoption law are very similar to our own.

The principle *adoptio naturam imitatur* bases several rules. Though an adopter need not be married, a *castratus* could not adopt, at least in later law. The adopter must be old enough to be the father, and Justinian fixed the difference at 18 years ... Women, being incapable of *patria potestas*, could not adopt in classical law. In an interpolated constitution dated a.d. 291 Diocletian is said to have allowed adoption as a consolation to a woman who had lost her children, and Justinian accepted this as the rule ... [10]

Adoption was not strictly necessary under Roman law, for it was possible to appoint an heir by testament. Buckland remarks that 'the will is originally nomination of a successor in the chieftaincy of the group', and says that it is possibly an older idea than that of hereditary sovereignty.

Well known as adoption was in Rome (and some historians have suggested that one reason for its popularity was the aversion of upper-class Roman women to childbearing), there are other societies of the ancient world in which adoption was *de rigueur*.

The country most widely known for its ancestor cult is China, and unsurprisingly, adoption flourished there too. Anthropologists have evolved plausible theories about the mechanism of Chinese ancestor worship, combining psychology and economics.

One recent hypothesis is that those who benefit from someone's death (i.e. receive an inheritance) are likely to feel guilty over the possibility that they wished for the death. To expiate this guilt, they perform rites of worship to the dead. The school of thought founded by Maurice Freedman takes this further in a practical direction. One of his students said of Taiwan, where the ancestor cult continues almost unchanged:

> In studying the reciprocity that is at the heart of ancestor worship, we shall find that the living are expected to care for the dead in payment of the debts they owe them. Beyond this, in the act of meeting this obligation, the living hope to inspire a further reciprocal response from the ancestors, to obtain through them the good life as they perceive it: wealth, rich harvests, and offspring who will ensure undying memory and sustenance in the afterlife.[11]

To have one's tablet placed in the hall of ancestors, one must have a descendant to place it there. Although it is possible to appoint a descendant, a nephew for example, or even to leave one's property to a complete stranger in return for worship, the usual practice of the childless is adoption.

The Chinese preference for sons, whether natural or adopted, has often been misinterpreted. It is not that men have all the power in the family, or that they are considered the only useful members of it. Mothers and mothers-in-law have enormous power in traditional Chinese families, especially after they have borne sons. The problem with daughters is that they are only temporary members of the lineage into which they are born.

> A woman's stay in her natal home is usually temporary, ending when she marries out of it. From her birth it is expected that she will give the children she bears and her adult labor to the family of her husband ... She has no right at all to care or worship from the members of her natal lineage because she is not a permanently committed member of that lineage. She was born to leave it.[12]

Since an unmarried woman, unless she has been betrothed, must have a tablet in the hall for unmarried girls, she may be posthumously married.

The adopted child in China is thus almost always a boy, and almost always goes to a childless (or at least sonless) family. But if his natural parents lose their other children after he is adopted, he may find that he has to worship both sets of parents.

There is one circumstance, however, in which girls are adopted — a girl may become a *sim-pua*, or 'little daughter-in-law'. She is adopted in early childhood, and it is intended that she should marry her foster-brother, or at least some male member of the lineage into which she is adopted. One anthropologist in Shantung in the 1930s found that 35 per cent of the girls in the families he studied had been adopted in this way — the poverty of the depression years had induced families to part early with daughters who would be leaving them anyway in due course.

This relates adoption to the exchange of women in marriage, which many anthropologists, following Claude Lévi-Strauss, now believe to be the most basic element in the creation of human society. It also provides a link between the Eurasian societies we are considering and tribal society, in both of which adoption is clearly a form of exchange.

Lévi-Strauss studied both kinds of society in formulating the theory that he evolved as a solution to the problem of incest, long considered the least explicable of human taboos. The survival and cohesion of the group, he found, depended on the degree to which the exchange of women created links with neighbouring groups: 'Make love not war.' If women stayed in their natal group, the consequence could be a dangerous isolation and diminishing of numbers. As one South American Indian said to him, 'Why would you marry your sister? Don't you want a brother-in-law?'

Lévi-Strauss eventually combined his theories of incest and exogamy into a generalized explanation of human marriage taboos.

> incest proper, and its metaphorical form as the violation of a minor (by someone 'old enough to be her father', as the expression goes), even combines in some countries, with its direct opposite, inter-racial sexual relations, an extreme form of exogamy, as the two most powerful inducements to horror and collective vengeance.[13]

The significance of this line of thought for the interpretation of adoption will become even clearer as we see its continuing relation to other forms of kinship. It is enough at this point to say that the Chinese custom of daughter-in-law adoption has parallels in other societies. Margaret Mead's study of the Arapesh, for example, revealed that a young man would provide food for a little girl as a way of singling her out as his future bride and establishing a claim on her. One of the South American tribes studied by Lévi-Strauss allowed a man to 'adopt' a little girl with the same goal in mind — as the anthropologist remarked, this confusion of marriage and parenthood would be viewed in our society as the worst of sins.

The question of exogamy is also relevant to adoption. In the southern United States, adoption across racial lines, like inter-racial marriage, has traditionally been forbidden. The question of whether adoption of a close relative is prescribed or forbidden varies as much around the world as does that other favourite theme of the anthropologists, cross-cousin marriage. Relative adoption is at present viewed with suspicion by many Western experts: they speak of the confusion the child will experience if he has two relationships to the same person. But among the Polynesians, adoption of anyone but a relative is considered an insult to the extended family.

Adoption across too many class lines is, likewise, too extreme a form of exogamy for most societies to take—some movement upwards does usually occur, and provides the raison d'être for many adoptions, but it is strictly limited by custom. Adopters in our own day are warned, for example, that a child from a much lower social class is unlikely to come up to their high intellectual expectations of it; the 'matching' done by adoption agencies is done on an implicit class basis.

It has been assumed in the West that Asian preference for relative adoption was one of the reasons why the children of foreign soldiers (in Korea and Vietnam for example) were often unacceptable in their own societies. But this is a simplification: the case of India demonstrates that there are mechanisms for the legitimation of any child born to an Asian woman.

Hindu India is famous for adoption—Mayne's *Treatise on Hindu Law* devotes over a hundred pages to it, and traditional commentaries on the law have identified no fewer than twelve types of adoption. The degree of closeness of adopter and adoptee is thoroughly prescribed in Hindu law. It is an established principle that the adopted boy should be 'the reflection of a son'—as similar as possible to a natural child. It is preferable for him to be of the same family, but he must not be within the prohibited degrees of kinship. His mother must be someone the adopter could have married—i.e., not a sister or a daughter. He must be of the same caste as the adopter, even if he is unrelated.

Although funeral rites and ancestor worship are important to the Hindus, Mayne suggests that secular motives for adoption are perhaps the dominant ones. As in China, 'the funeral cake follows the family name and the estate'—in other words, funeral offerings are a return for an inheritance. But perhaps the whole debate over motives is unnecessary: 'adoption itself is in all cases for the continuance of the line and for the perpetuation of the family name, whether the motives are secular or religious.'[14]

Adoption, as a form of exchange, must be transacted between

the adopter and the adoptee's parents. Hence the provision, so curious to Westerners, that an orphan cannot be adopted — there is no one to give him in adoption.

One of the reasons for the desire for a personal heir is the immensely complicated Hindu law of inheritance. If a man dies intestate or without appointing an heir, all his property must be left, according to the rules, in decreasing percentages as the heirs get more distant. The property, especially if it is land, may be divided into parcels too small to be of use to anyone; an appointed heir will at least receive an intact estate.

The twelve sorts of sons identified by Hindu law can be reduced to two — natural and adopted. The legitimate son comes first in preference, and obviates the need for any other sort. But a man with nothing but daughters may appoint a daughter to have a son that he later claims as his own. Thus men are advised not to marry a girl without brothers, for their sons may be taken by the girl's father.

The wife may have a son by another man, and the child can then be legitimated by her husband. This can be done secretly, almost as a form of artificial insemination — but the legal commentaries advise that a man be careful that all forms and disclaimers are properly observed, or the genitor may have a claim to the child. This debate is presently going on in the West over the question of donor insemination — what is the legal status of the child?

The son of an unmarried daughter still living in her father's house can be adopted by the girl's father; in fact it seems that legally it is his child, since he is still the guardian of the girl.

These are all, strictly speaking, types of natural son. There are also several different types of adopted son. Not only can a boy be given or sold by his parents; if he is old enough, he can give himself in adoption with his parents' consent.

Only a man who has none of the types of natural son will adopt; but many of the Hindu 'natural' sons would be called adopted sons in other cultures. What degree of kinship determines whether a son is natural or adopted? If he has any of the adoptive father's blood at all, Hindu law would consider him a natural son.

The levirate of ancient Hebrew law finds an interesting

36

parallel in the Hindu custom of widow adoption, whereby a woman can be empowered by her husband to adopt sons after his death, who will then be legally considered his sons.

There is only one way of adopting girls under Hindu law: the dancing girls of Madras and Pondicherry were allowed to adopt daughters to follow their profession and inherit their property. This is reminiscent of the adoption by Babylonian craftsmen (and European guildsmen) of their successors; but because it is the only instance in which women were their own masters and employers, it is the only case in which they could adopt as if they were heads of households.

Under Indian law, a man could not adopt his own illegitimate son; but this is clearly because the owner of the mother had the title to the child. A woman belonged first to her father and then to her husband; her lover had no legal claim on her, and thus none on the child.

The big changes in Hindu law came about as a result of English rule. There were many provisions in the law of adoption that seemed curious, even ridiculous, to the English—such as the rule against the adoption of orphans, just the people who might be thought to need it most. The 'sale' of children is the aspect of adoption that the British found most shocking in many parts of their empire; but as in the case of the African bride-price (another parallel between marriage and adoption) they often misinterpreted the facts.

The parents of the child given in adoption, in India as elsewhere, often have many children; they are seeking an opportunity for the child by allying him (and therefore themselves) with a richer or higher-status family. It is usual for them to receive something tangible in return; but this does not alter the fact that they are thinking primarily of the child when they arrange the adoption. They are trying to prevent too much division of the scarce resources they will be able to leave their children, and to give one at least of the children an opportunity to do better for himself. As Mayne remarks, 'Paupers have souls to be saved, but they are not in the habit of adopting.'

Western insistence on the child-rescue aspect of adoption has led to hypocrisy: instead of giving the child in adoption to rich foreigners, an Asian mother may now use the subterfuge of abandoning it to an orphanage, so that it can be adopted as an 'orphan'. The open recognition that it is the rich who adopt the children of the poor may be distasteful to modern sensibilities, but concealing the facts does not alter them.

Adoption by foreigners, however, is a recent addition to the Asian scene, and coexists with traditional heir-adoption. The ancient Eurasian pattern can be traced in Rome, China, and India—all societies with a certain amount of population pressure on the land, with a religion of fertility and ancestor worship, and with unilineal descent groups. These elements are so intertwined that it is difficult to isolate any one of them as the determinant of adoption practice; but the picture we get of the whole inheritance pattern in the three societies is similar, and adoption is a necessary part of it.

We have contrasted these settled, landholding societies with the nomadic peoples of the Middle East, who created the transcendent religions appropriate to weather-conscious herdsmen in conditions of scarcity. The all-seeing eye of the desert sky god could penetrate such flimsy fictions as adoption; the matter of keeping the blood lines of feuding tribes distinct made any such device antipathetic; and having a personal heir did not matter so much when such property as there was took the form of cattle.

These two traditions have together formed much of modern European thinking about adoption, while the vast differences between them have caused many anomalies. There is a third, more obscure, strand in the story, whose beginnings are difficult to see clearly.

Until they invaded the Roman Empire, the tribes of northern Europe were only vaguely known by the civilized Mediterranean peoples; and much about their early social organization is lost to us. The major difference between them and the other societies we have looked at seems to be that, like the similarly nomadic and warlike Zulus, they were organized by age-group rather than by family. Blood-brotherhood was the form of fictive kinship most practised by the Norsemen (interestingly, it is also mentioned as a form of adoption among the pre-Islamic Arabs). There is no evidence that the adoption of children was practised by these people—indeed, one suspects that if it had been, there would be some evidence of it in the traditions of their descendants. Chiefs were chosen by trials of

38

strength, and the chief was thought of as a father to his people. The idea that the whole society formed a family influenced the development of European feudalism.

The collapse of the Roman Empire, and the collision between Nordic and Mediterranean culture, created such chaos that what social organization there was took primitive forms. Far from developing sophisticated notions like adoption, the product of long-settled societies with well-established means of preserving themselves, early Medieval Europe was a jungle of warring chiefs, whose legitimacy was established by conquest and perpetuated by force.

The family was, however, the prototype of social organization even here, and other social forms followed it. In fact, the relation of the vassal to his feudal lord was very like that of adoptee to adopter in China: a typical form of ritual homage was 'I become your man in respect of the tenement which I hold of you'.

Although the obligations arising from blood-relationship played a very active part in [feudal society], it did not rely on kinship alone. More precisely, feudal ties proper were developed when those of kinship proved inadequate.[15]

Property was held only for a man's lifetime; then it reverted to the feudal chief, who appointed the next incumbent. There was some property that passed to a man's heirs (and during the Middle Ages this proportion was gradually increased), but the heirs were prescribed and were not a matter of personal choice. Where the estate was indivisible, primogeniture was used to select the heir. There was no place for adoption in this strict system, where only the chief had enough freedom of action to decide on the disposition of property. Even he, to preserve his legitimacy, had to succeed through the blood line.

The feudal system was introduced to England at the time of the Norman Conquest.

From the point of view of English law, the whole country became the property of the Crown, and allodial estates, over which the proprietor exercised full and unrestricted ownership, did not exist.[16]

39

This heritage is still to be found in England, in the entailed estates and titles that may not pass to adopted children, or indeed to anyone but the heir prescribed by law.

The method of choosing the heir, as set out in Blackstone's commentaries, was to look for the *parentela*, or the direct next-generation descendants of one man, and then for the individual heir within the *parentela*. If a man himself had no descendants, his heir would be sought first from among his father's descendants, then among his grandfather's, and so on back to Adam if necessary. The law's distinction between 'real' (or landed) and 'personal' property dictated that the first could not be willed, but that the latter must be willed. Not until the Administration of Estates Act, 1925, could a man's chosen representative be the trustee for his entire estate, including land. Is it a coincidence that this law was passed the year before the first English Adoption Act?

The legacy of feudalism has not entirely disappeared today; but the long period of transition between the Germanic past and the modern era, during which adoption became increasingly possible in a part of the world to which it was not native, has been going on since the Middle Ages. As Aries describes it:

> The modern way of life is the result of the divorce between elements which had formerly been united: friendship, religion, profession. It is also the result of the suppression of some of them, such as friendship and religion, and of the development of another element to which the Middle Ages attributed only secondary importance: the family.[17]

The feeling of belonging—and practical support—of the kind now given by the family was, in Medieval times, the role of the age group (for example in the case of students and apprentices), the professional group (guilds), or the Church (religious orders). Families themselves were extended not only by distant relatives, but by retainers of all kinds—nurses, vassals, pages, and so on. We will come back to this theme when we trace the emergence of adoption in Europe. At the moment, we will simply contrast feudal organization, the state as family, with the societies in which the extended family itself is almost a state.

The ties of kinship have been strongest and most extensive in primitive societies. Early Eurasian cultures—in Greece, Rome, China and India—also emphasized the extended family. But the seemingly primitive emphasis on the blood tie that characterized Medieval Europe was of a different kind. Social life was too fragmented and uncertain for such deliberate arrangements as adoption; lineage and blood kinship became all-important. The 'individualism' that led the West to explore, conquer, and industrialize the world arose from such restless and unsettled conditions—thus the non-adopters gradually gained influence over the adopters.

In time, however, the nomadic non-adopters, the heirs of European feudalism and the Judaeo-Christian tradition, constructed settled societies of their own. As the pace of disruptive social change was followed by attempts to make the new societies more cohesive, the need for adoption again became apparent.

Although the heir adoption of the classical cultures has all but disappeared from the modern world, primitive adoption in all its forms still exists. Indeed, it may be experiencing something of a revival, as the dislocations of industrial society are more clearly identified and as they begin to be rejected. Today, when the isolated individualism of the West is seen to be a cause of so many of our discontents, it is worth taking another look at how the extended family worked when it was part of a homogeneous society.

The anthropologists who first studied what they defined as primitive societies were often struck by the widespread sharing of parental roles. Some observers described this as adoption; others, when faced with the same phenomena, declared that adoption was unknown in the societies they were studying. There was no systematic distinction between adoption and fostering, and the situation has only recently begun to be cleared up. Jack Goody has outlined a new basis for theory:

> I have contrasted the role of adoption in modern western countries with the part it plays in 'traditional' Eurasian societies. But the position in tropical Africa stood out in great contrast to both. In the first place differences of status and wealth were small by comparison with Eurasia;

there was little intensive agriculture ... Land was relatively abundant and was little improved, either by terracing
or irrigation; water had to be scooped up, weights man-
handled ... and the land cultivated with the hoe.[18]

The abundance of land meant that there was little fear of
dividing an inheritance; the labour-intensive farming methods
meant that an extra member of the family was always welcome.
Thus although a man did not need to adopt in order to ensure
his personal continuity, children were highly valued and
competition for them was keen.

This places the form taken by adoption into context of the
economic organization of society, and helps to explain many
previously baffling discrepancies in the observations brought
back by anthropologists. In fact adoption on the tropical
African model is found throughout the primitive world, and it
provides some fundamental insights into what every society
means by parenthood.

What in fact is meant by a primitive society? It is often
asserted that no such thing exists today, and many so-called
primitive societies were on their way out even when they were
first studied by anthropologists — purists would even argue that
contact with an outside observer was in itself enough to distort
the reality of what he was studying. Perhaps there is nowhere in
the world now that is uncontaminated by contact with industrial
society; the primitive is almost a metaphorical way of speaking.

Ideally, a primitive society is preliterate, lives by herding,
gathering, and simple agriculture, is unmechanised and has a
homogeneous culture. Ritual is more important than inno-
vation; group cohesiveness more important than individualism.

One distinguishing mark of most primitive societies is that
their languages identify classes of kin where we would identify
individuals. As Radcliffe-Brown puts it, 'In primitive society
there is a strongly marked tendency to merge the individual in
the group to which he or she belongs.'[19]

Evans-Pritchard explains:

As is well known, in primitive societies there are any
number of persons a child calls and to some extent acts
towards and thinks of as 'father', 'mother', 'brother' and

'sister'; and these people are generally living in close proximity to him, so that from his infancy he sees them every day and learns to regard them as members of his 'family', in the wider sense ... There is not, therefore, the same emotional concentration on a tiny circle of persons.[20]

This is called by anthropologists 'classificatory terminology'. Radcliffe-Brown and Forde offer a definition:

The main principle of classificatory terminology is a simple one. If A and B are two brothers and X stands in a certain relationship to A, then he is regarded as standing in a somewhat similar relation to B. Similarly if A and B are two sisters ... The father's brother is called 'father' and the mother's sister is called 'mother'.[21]

Early anthropologists thought that such locutions proved that primitives did not know who their own parents were, since all their aunts and uncles were called by these names too. They said that perhaps 'group marriage' was historically prior to individual marriage, and the languages were still at the earlier stage.

We know now that classificatory terms reflect a social reality, but not quite that suggested by the early observers. More important than the identification with the nuclear family, which is of course overwhelmingly what we ourselves mean by the family, is the solidarity and unity of the entire kin group. Where survival depends on the ability of any number of people to fill parental roles, there are sophisticated mechanisms for detaching the child from his own parents and making him in some sense the child of the entire group. Adoption is the term that has often been used for these mechanisms, but it is so unlike what we mean by adoption that Esther Goody, who has studied the primitive system of child-exchange in great detail, calls it kinship fostering.

To understand the primitive tribal notion of adoption, we must first understand the tribal attitude to property. A recent visitor to Tanzania observed that 'It is an African tradition to regard land as a resource, not as property—no more fit to be owned than, in our eyes, a square mile of the sea.'[22]

It is worth noting that the region where adoption is most popular, Oceania, consists of a series of scattered islands—most of the property that provides the wealth of this society is in fact sea.

We will see how this attitude, a sort of natural socialism (which recent African leaders have made much of), goes with a family system extended beyond limits ever envisioned in the West; the ever-smaller nuclear family, with its consequent difficulty in absorbing new members, is the natural partner of capitalism.

To create a new family, a man must lay claim to his wife in a tangible way. Often this involves the paying of a bride-price; in some areas, the woman is not fully transferred from her old kin group to the new one until she has borne her first child.

Some societies in Sumatra and other parts of the Malay Archipelago have two kinds of marriage. If a full marriage payment is made the children belong to the father; we may call this a father-right marriage. But if no payment is made the children belong to the mother and her kin, the marriage being one of mother-right.[23]

In any case, there is a sense in which both kin-groups have some claim on children of the marriage, and the balance may be tipped in favour of the group that pays. This attitude extends to adoption.

In the Banks Islands payment of the midwife's fee is sufficient to establish adoptive claim to a child. If the husband of the natural mother cannot afford the fee or happens to be away at the time, another man is likely to arrogate paternity. This practice of paying the medical expenses of the natural mother in return for custody of the child is remarkably similar to practice in non-agency adoptions in the United States.[24]

In tribal society, the more members a family had, the better. It meant more hands to help with the work, and productivity was limited by the number of people available to till the soil, carry water, and so on, not by the amount of land

44

available. Polygamy was practised in most of these societies, or at least serial monogamy. A woman and her small children formed a social group independent of the male, who had certain duties towards them which were often shared by the male members of the woman's own clan.

Marriage in such societies was often seen as a conflict between two groups of kin. Wives could and would return home on the slightest provocation, and when it came to fostering, the mother's brother usually had first claim on the children.

The curious but extremely widespread institution of cross-cousin marriage has been seen as one way round this difficulty. Esther Goody reports of the Gonja of northern Ghana: 'The reason always given for preferring marriage to a kinswoman is that should there be a divorce, the children will not be lost to the husband since the wife is also a relative.'[25] Sometimes the prescribed wife is on the mother's side, sometimes on the father's; but while cross-cousins (the children of a brother and sister) are often enjoined to marry, parallel cousins (the children of two brothers or two sisters) are usually forbidden to do so.

This indicates that incest taboos are not behind such marriage prohibitions, at least not in the sense that the genetic results of incest are feared. The prohibited cousins are of the same degree of consanguinity as the prescribed cousins. Thus Lévi-Strauss is probably closer to the truth in his analysis of exogamy:

> exogamy has a value less negative than positive, that it asserts the social existence of other people, and that it prohibits endogamous marriage only in order to introduce, and to prescribe, marriage with a group other than the biological family, certainly not because a biological danger is attached to consanguineous marriage, but because exogamous marriage results in a social benefit.[26]

Why, then, is the cross-cousin preferred, since he is already a relative? Some of this probably has to do with the special relationship of mother's brothers and sister's sons in patriarchal societies.

This particular uncle is often seen as the protector of his sister against her husband, and the protector of her children against their father. He is the representative of the claims of the mother's side of the family.

In patrilineal society, the father is the authority figure—the source of rules, legitimacy, and discipline. The mother represents the affectionate side of family life. By extension, her brother represents affection too—in any case, in the view of anthropologists, both affection and discipline cannot come from the same person, and a division of the functions between father and uncle relieves some of the possible tensions in the family group.

In African societies, a 'joking relationship', in which any sort of teasing, irreverence, and game is permissible, exists between a boy and his maternal uncle and between a boy and his grandfather. These are, not coincidentally, the two relatives preferred when it comes to kinship fostering. The constraints of formality that exist with the father are relaxed with the next generation up and with the males of the mother's family, so these are often chosen to provide the upbringing that is too intimate to be compatible with the dignity of fatherhood.

Some observers of kinship fostering have described it in a way that contradicts the notion of strict father/indulgent uncle. These see the nuclear family itself as too affectionate and indulgent to train the child properly in the tasks of life, necessitating sending him away during his formative years to be toughened by a relative who will not feel the parents' temptation to spoil him.

Both these explanations of fostering, however, attempt to interpret it as a kind of apprenticeship, and concentrate on its psychological effect on the child. The truth probably is that the fostering system is 'about' the creation and preservation of the entire society—its message to the individual is that his role is a subordinate one; his fate is linked with, but less important than, the fate of the group. In this it is like exogamy. Sending one's children to be fostered, and receiving children from other kin, is like the exchange of daughters and sisters as wives. As Lévi-Strauss has said:

The total relationship of exchange which constitutes marriage is not established between a man and a woman, where each owes and receives something, but between two

46

groups of men, and the woman figures only as one of the objects in the exchange, not as one of the partners between whom the exchange takes place.[27]

Similarly, the child who is fostered is an object of exchange, not one of the parties to it.

In such societies, quarrels are likely to arise over who is to keep the children, not over who is inescapably responsible for the burden of their support.

How widespread an institution is kinship fostering? At times it seems to approach universality:

> In the Gilbert Islands the persons who pass for a man or a woman's parents are never the real parents, for it is an inevitable rule that every child is adopted at birth by foster-parents ... Very poor people have sometimes difficulty in finding adoptive parents for their children, and may suffer the mortification of having to bring up their own children.[28]

Modern methods of quantification have related such an ideal model to what really happens; but certainly it seems to be true that in some of the islands of Oceania, the proportion of children fostered in this way is as high as 80 per cent. In Central Africa, it never seems to be more than about 30 per cent.

Esther Goody's description of Ghanaian practice is perhaps the most complete that exists of this institution, and it is worth quoting at length.

> There is a widespread custom in Gonja of fostering the children of siblings and of one's own children. This means that from the age of six or seven, usually until marriage, a child may be reared by a parent's sibling or grandparent, living with them rather than with his own parents. Throughout the fostering period, visits are exchanged, the foster child returning for short periods to see his parents, while they and his siblings visit him. The diffuse claims on children of a marriage and the reciprocal claims of the children on their dispersed kin are aspects of the custom of fostering ... This is not, as might at first appear, a form of

47

adoption, for adoption as it is usually defined involves a
legal change in status of the adoptee, which is specifically
not the case in Gonja. Unlike adoption, fostering by kin
involves no permanent forfeiting of rights or duties in order
to assume a new set, no change in the kinship terms used
between the people involved, and no permanent change of
status in any sense ... In societies where adoption is
regularly practised, as in classical Indian and Chinese
cultures, ancient Rome, and today in rural Japan, the
explicit intention is that by conferring membership on a
selected individual, the continuity of the group, whether
represented by ancestral shrines, name and titles, or
economic assets, may be secured. But the institution of
kinship fostering cannot act in this way.[29]

This is not entirely true of all varieties of kinship fostering. The
confusion with adoption is greater in some societies, notably in
Polynesia, where there is no really clear dividing line. There,
too, kin are preferred for fostering or adoption, and the real
parents are known to the adopters. Previous parental ties may
even be kept up by the children. There is widespread feeling
against fostering or adopting from outside the kin group.

But the adopted child often inherits as if he were the natural
child of his adopters; he often takes their name. Indeed, the
introduction of modern Western law into Polynesia has had
some confusing, rather than clarifying, effects on the whole
procedure. In Tahiti, for example, a child would be chosen for
adoption before his birth, and would take the name of the
adoptive parents immediately, although no effort would be
made to conceal his true parentage. But with the advent of
French colonial law, it became necessary to register the birth.
In keeping with traditional practice, the adoptive parents
would register the birth in their own names—an act which was
illegal under French law.

It is probably safe to say that the younger the child when
adopted, the more complete his change of status. By Polynesian
standards, adoption or fostering in Gonja takes place late in the
child's life, and is more associated with training in the tasks of
adulthood than with nurturing an infant. Polynesians often
arrange an adoption before the child's birth, and although it

may stay with its mother during the period of lactation, artificial feeding methods have made an earlier transfer possible.

There are many overt motives for kinship fostering (although they are all subordinate to the overriding 'exchange' motive). The example of colonial Uganda provides an unusually clear breakdown of these motives. A child could go to the father's brother—in this case the motive was to give him a strict training (as usual, this is the province of the father's side of the family). He might be sent to a relative who happened to be a chief; this, it was hoped, would provide for his later advancement in life. A girl, too, could be sent to the chief—this time as a future bride. Grandparents and other relatives could also foster a child, especially if they had few or none in the household; in this case, care and training were exchanged for the child's labour. Unlike adoption, kinship fostering could accommodate children of both sexes, and be done by relatives whose own children had grown up and left home or were all of one sex. A girl to help in the houschold was as valuable as a boy to help in the fields.

> Thus one can trace two separate motives for the practice which are not necessarily always in harmony. One is interest in the child's own future and the wish to secure him a sound upbringing and opportunities of advancement. The other lies in the recognition of mutual obligations between relatives and a desire to strengthen the bonds of kinship in a concrete manner.[30]

In 1934, when this account was written, many of these practices had been stopped by Christian missionaries, but children might still be sent to a relative who lived near the district school—thus the old ways adapted to new practicalities.

The issue of the midwife's payment is raised in a new way in Uganda—the mother's brother was considered to have an inherent right to her children, and although he could not be refused one or two for fostering, he had to be paid for each child he was not given. The fostering system is in many societies a sort of tug-of-war between the mother's and the father's kin, with children going alternately to each side of the family. When a marriage breaks up, it is perhaps an indication that the pull of the kin group has proved stronger than the marriage tie.

What is in fact the psychological message of fostering? How can this system be related to the Western notion of family life, in which the voluntary relinquishing of children by a married couple would be regarded with horror?

A recent description of Polynesian adoption argues that:

> The message in the Polynesian and Micronesian adoption is that RELATIONSHIPS BETWEEN ALL PARENTS AND CHILDREN ARE FRAGILE AND CONDITIONAL. The form of Western adoption mutes from community awareness the impact of the breaking of the biological relationship and thus protects the essential Western orientation that RELATIONSHIPS BETWEEN ALL PARENTS AND CHILDREN ARE CATEGORICAL.[31]

This means that in Polynesia, adoption is *supposed* to happen. In the West, the preservation of the biological family is the ideal; adoption is *not* supposed to happen. Every effort is made to duplicate the biological family when adoption occurs; secrecy often surrounds the fact itself. In Oceania, to adopt is easier than to keep one's own children. In fact to keep a child, parents may have to risk offending their kin and cutting themselves off from normal social life. The person who raises the child always expects and usually receives the child's love and gratitude, because he competed with many other claimants for the task.

Experiencing parent–child relationships as conditional, especially in the context of the particularly warm and secure infancy enjoyed by the child in a primitive society, throws him off balance—he has a sudden and brutal awakening to the fact that the people to whom he has become so closely attached are ready to hand him over to what are, to him, perfect strangers.

The message he receives is: don't trust anyone unreservedly, for this experience may be repeated. Friendship, even the closest, is contingent on polite and hospitable behaviour; marriage is the same. This helps to make social life easier in the wider society; misbehaviour is not tolerated, let alone the kind of aggression that can be practised in our society without necessarily breaking family ties.

Western orthodoxy now holds that this is exactly the sort of experience that produces anti-social adults. This apparent paradox can only be resolved by studying all the child's emotional experiences in detail, and seeing how they fit into society's expectations of him. Extremely nurturant behaviour on the part of adults, followed by traumatic separation, may 'balance out' in a way not very different from the continuous care, combining discipline and affection, that Western children receive.

The strains of Western family life, as evidenced in adolescent rebellion and sibling rivalry, for example, are due partly to the categorical nature of kin relationships. Perhaps these are alleviated in societies where kin relationships are easily changed. As an observer of the Tangu of New Guinea found:

No household wants children who do not show their appreciation in affection and services, and, since there is no family name and no lineage to perpetuate, a perverse child is allowed to find its most suitable and satisfactory ambience.[32]

Many observers have commented that the loading of all possible parental roles—nurturing, discipline, daily care, socialization, support, and so on—on to the biological parents alone has created strains unmatched in any other sort of family. There are no longer grandparents, servants, or extended kin to share the burden. And when adoption does take place, it is a difficult and total shifting of all these roles on to the new parents.

Kinship fostering, although it sometimes approaches the total nature of Western adoption, also shows the way to a sharing of parental roles, something that is increasingly widely advocated in our society.

The psychological effects of kinship fostering depend for their efficacy on the preservation of the society's integrity. When the traditional pattern begins to break up, inappropriate parts of it may survive in new situations. This has been happening in many parts of the primitive world. One society uses fostering, another adoption, another polygamy: it is impossible to trace the creation of homogeneous societies and to show how each arrived at its particular balance; but it is all too easy to see how they become unbalanced when new elements are suddenly added.

The breaking up of a homogeneous culture creates many areas of strain. English social workers are familiar with West Indian families practising their traditional form of kinship fostering, the raising of children by their grandmother. But a new element has been added: the parents' migration to England, to send back enough money to support the family and to enable the children to eventually join the parents. This system works well at home, where the children's contact with the parents is not severed; but the 16-year-old child arriving in London to live with a mother he hasn't seen since infancy is subjected to a strain that many find intolerable.

Equally, the child of African students in London may be fostered for some years. The parents, having completed their studies, ask for his return on their departure for home. The child does not know them—far from being fostered by kin, he has been living in a totally different culture. The parents do not realize that their traditional pattern has been radically changed. This theme recurs in every discussion of the problems of inter-racial adoption in the West.

African countries attempting to set up social welfare systems face many of the same problems. Insistence on legal adoption may destroy the system of kinship fostering and replace it with institutions much more damaging to the children—Western-style orphanages, for example.

A noteworthy aspect of development in West Africa has been the tendency to treat social problems in the same way as the economy is treated, i.e. by the importation of European models and know-how. Mental hospitals are established to deal with psychiatric troubles: remand homes are introduced to deal with recalcitrant youths: state pension schemes are worked out to deal with the aged, and adoption laws are formulated to safeguard the interests of the parties concerned. In universities, social administration courses are started by expatriate staff on expatriate lines, using handbooks written for social workers in Brooklyn or Birmingham.[33]

Nationalism, and a clearer view of the possibilities open to them, is leading many developing countries to reject the 'expatriate' model; and the admiration many Westerners feel for the traditional methods of these countries indicates that they may be wise to do so.

Still, there are ways in which the inexorable forces of social change cannot help but dislocate traditional forms. In Hawaii, the generation gap causes difficulties between modern parents who want to keep their own children, and old-fashioned grandparents who want to foster or adopt them. This kind of example can be multiplied many times over.

The United States is in fact the scene of a collision between the Judaeo-Christian tradition, with all that that means in the way of difficult adoption, and the tribal kinship-fostering patterns of its peripheral groups. The WASP majority seems incapable of learning from the strengths of its neighbours, who are in any case busy emulating the ruling group.

What can modern man learn from the static, enclosed societies we call primitive? How can he use the relaxed flexibility of the extended family, and the easy sharing of children, without losing the dynamic range of possibilities he so prizes? One thing he can try to learn is how to repair the damage done by his kind of society, and his gradual embracing of adoption represents this kind of learning.

The inflexibility and heartlessness associated with the period of Western expansion are reflected in the characteristics of the nuclear family. An intensely protective refuge from a competitive world, it has also been a forcing-house of the qualities needed to succeed in that world. Any diminution of its power may indicate that society at large is becoming more humane, ready to protect its members from the worst consequences of their relationships with each other. As we trace the rise of adoption in the West, perhaps we can see this process at work.

53

3 The Rebirth of Adoption

Blue blood! Blue blood!
Of what avail art thou
To serve us now?
Though dating from the Flood,
Blue blood!
W. S. Gilbert, *Iolanthe*

Against a background of hierarchical societies where adoption was well-known, and tribal societies where kinship fostering took its place, we can see how anomalous were the several centuries during which the Anglo-Saxon world, and much of Western Europe, practised no form of legal adoption at all.

Rapid social change is one explanation of this: the collapse of the Roman Empire made practices like adoption, very much the product of a coherent social order, give way to the supremacy of blood ties and feudal bonds. Not until industrial capitalism was well established, and had begun repairing the ravages of its early years, did adoption appear again on the European scene.

The 'dark ages' of adoption may have begun at the same time as the European Dark Ages, with the fall of Rome in 476. Although many ancient ideas were rediscovered by the Renaissance, adoption was not reinstated in continental Europe until the French Revolution, and in the English-speaking countries until about the end of the nineteenth century. Adoption may have occurred during this long 'dark age', but because it was *de facto* rather than *de jure*, we have no way of knowing its extent. Families had recourse to other ways of perpetuating themselves; and other provisions had to be made for children without families.

To some extent, feudal society replaced the family by the system of vassalage; and the Christian Church was originally unfavourable to adoption. What remained of extended-kin networks in Europe and its colonies was gradually and systematically destroyed by capitalism—at least among the white population—and a money economy, under which most people were employees, took its place. The extended family became a liability instead of a necessity, and children a drain on the family's income rather than an addition to it.

Feudal society had ways of taking care of its own, but for those who fell through this rather loose net there was one other recourse: the Church. Religious orders were open to those who belonged nowhere else, and one of their historic functions was the rescue of fallen women and homeless children.

The monastic orders, being celibate, could only perpetuate themselves by adoption, so to speak—conversion to the religious 'family' was the recruiting method used by religious orders throughout their history.

The Medieval Church was, in a way, the mirror of feudal society; the feudal lord had his 'family' and the abbot or bishop had his. Both were, of course, forms of fictive kinship; but instead of supplementing the natural family, they competed with it.

Becoming a monk, nun, or priest—in other words, being adopted by the Church—has always had strict rules and initiation rituals; by contrast, the Church has throughout its history given few rules for the family conduct of its lay members. The sacraments are the points of contact between the ordinary christian and the dogmas of the Church; but they do not cover day-to-day experience.

The Church has always been primarily concerned with maintaining and increasing its membership. The sacraments are designed to keep people in the Church and to ensure that the rest of the family joins them there. Communion is the reaffirmation of membership; marriage is only performed, ideally, between two Church members—if one of the partners is a non-member, he is urged to convert, or at least promise to bring the children up in the faith. Wherever the Church touches family life, its main concern is its own survival, and everything it enjoins on its membership follows from this.

This substitution of the religious family for the secular one has led to some conflicts, but it has also made the Church very flexible in its response to different ways of organizing society. The legitimation of bastards on the marriage of their parents was part of canon law long before it was part of the common law of England, because it was a way of obtaining new members (illegitimate people could not be Church members, because they were outside society altogether). The 'rescue' of fallen women was part of Church work long before the rest of society would have anything to do with them; again, this was to the Church's advantage, because it meant that they would stay within the Church's jurisdiction

Naturally, orphans and abandoned children figured early and prominently in the history of the Church's social work. Today, they still fill Church orphanages—and from there the religious orders—in many parts of the world.

Adoption has always been an equivocal act in the eyes of the Church. Although nowadays it is a recognized part of social welfare work, and as such accepted by the Church as well as by the secular agencies engaged in such work, it is hard to track down a specific Christian dictum on the subject.

All that can be said with certainty is that when adoption was likely to bring new Church members, it was approved; when it was likely to lose potential recruits, it was disapproved. Today, Church adoption agencies, especially Catholic ones, are unwilling to let children go to adopters outside the faith.

The decline of the power of the Church, and the growing involvement of the state in social welfare work, were the preconditions of modern adoption practice. We have traced the story as far as the Middle Ages, and we have seen how age groups, feudal and religious pseudo-families, and apprenticeship systems combined to take the pressure off the family itself as a socializing instrument. Aries says explicitly: 'The concept of the line was the only concept of a family character known to the Middle Ages ... It extended to the ties of blood without regard to the emotions engendered by cohabitation and intimacy.'[1] Typically, it was this society that practised primogeniture—the custom of leaving all the property to the eldest son. This is a notion that goes with a concept of the family as 'line' — a family based on intimate cohabitation practises the equality of siblings.

One of the great changes between the Middle Ages and our own day has been the invention of childhood itself as a distinctive phase. Aries shows how the very concept of the family

> was formed around the conjugal family, that of parents and children. This concept is closely linked to that of childhood. It has less and less to do with problems such as the honour of a line, the integrity of an inheritance, or the age and permanence of a name: it springs simply from the unique relationship between the parents and the children.[2]

The idea of conjugal family has never completely replaced notions of line and inheritance, but the balance has shifted steadily towards the former idea ever since the Middle Ages. Parents and children today spend more time as part of the same family than they did then; the dangers of infant mortality induced Medieval parents to push their children into the adult world as soon as possible, usually between the ages of 7 and 9.

Even before that age, children, particularly in the upper classes, were frequently fostered by relatives or by nurses. Wet-nursing was necessary for any child whose own mother could not feed it, but among the well-off it reached the status of an institution. After the nursing period, the child might be fostered by anyone who could be considered appropriate from the point of view of education, advantageous connection, or safety.

> In royal households ... although wet nurses were of lowly status, the children were subsequently looked after by titled gentlewomen. Earlier, during the middle ages, male children were often sent away from court to be brought up by strangers ... While the reasons behind such fostering certainly included dynastic security, the rearing of children by proxy parents was well established in Britain among this and other social strata long before the coming of the Foundling Hospital for the poor and the Public School for the rich.[3]

Putting children out to nurse was a custom that had its detractors; by the eighteenth century, Rousseau was attacking it on the grounds that women who avoided doing the job themselves were put off by over-civilized squeamishness.

Maternal deprivation during the nursing and fostering period is something we would be conscious of today, but it was not widely recognized at the time. It was, of course, possible for a child to receive more constant and loving care from his nurse than he would have received from his natural mother—a pattern that can be seen again in the nanny era. But Dr Johnson corroborates the suspicion that children put out to nurse were sometimes at risk physically and emotionally: he attributed his crippling melancholia to the sense of abandonment he felt when sent away from his mother to a careless and diseased nurse.

After the disintegration of the feudal system, under which everyone had a place somewhere in the hierarchy, and orphans were easily absorbed by the large aristocratic households, there was an interim period during which parentless children were nobody's responsibility. This is the period during which modern capitalism was establishing itself. In England, the attack on the Roman Church helped to destroy the Medieval order, and social problems that had been solved by Church and nobility were placed squarely at the door of the state.

The English experience has been widely influential because of the size of the British Empire. Because they illuminate today's practice around the world, the ideas developed in the early modern period in England are worth studying in some detail.

The first Poor Law in England was passed in 1597. Among the indigent for whom it made provision, abandoned, orphaned, and destitute children figured prominently.

In all sections of society ... the common practice was for children to leave the family environment early in life. In this respect, therefore, poor children who came under the aegis of these Acts were originally not treated very differently from children in other sections of the community, although the pattern established by statute in the sixteenth century involved untold misery for the children of the poor in later centuries, by which time, in other classes, separation of parents and children had been largely abandoned.[4]

The Tudor Poor Laws were partly a legacy of Medieval concern for the people under one's protection; but the fact that they were administered by the parishes, rather than centrally, meant that every parish attempted to keep its poor rate down by harrying the beneficiaries out of the district.

The use of the law to support indigent children was very strictly administered. Christian morality decreed, and rate-payers agreed, that the parents should be held responsible for such children if at all possible; bearing an illegitimate child carried a criminal sentence, and the mother could not leave the child in the care of the authorities without coming under their jurisdiction herself. Even when this did not mean prison, it certainly meant the workhouse: a fate that became notorious in history. 'The basic idea was to keep the poor rate low, which resulted in a system based on deterring those in need from using it.'[5] Not only were food and lodging of the most meagre kind, but families were separated: children were often housed in separate institutions until they were old enough for the men's and women's houses.

For 300 years, the Poor Laws were used as an instrument of class warfare. It was widely believed that the poor were eager to abandon their children and thus avoid responsibility for their support: thus the willingness of the authorities to care for them was hedged about with humiliating restrictions. As codified in 1834, the four principles of poor relief (which was only available to a man poorer than the poorest labourer, many of whom were themselves well below what we would call the 'poverty line') were:

1. The loss of personal reputation (the stigma of pauperism).
2. The loss of personal freedom (detention in the work-house).
3. The loss of political freedom (disenfranchisement).
4. Tasks in the workhouse selected as being both irksome and unskilled.

Thus the operation of the Poor Laws had the paradoxical effect of preventing anyone who once fell under their sway from ever again being financially independent.

Children who grew up in these institutions were typically both emotionally and physically unfit to lead a normal life. Adoption was not encouraged, as it would have been seen as an incentive to the irresponsible poor to abandon their children even more readily. The unmarried mother must bear the consequences of her act—consequences which were visited even more heavily on her child.

A witness to the 1909 Poor Law Commission testified:

> Semi-starvation is not a painful process and its victims do not recognize what is happening. The undernourished child is easily tired, and usually slow, dull and listless, but he is often not to his knowledge hungry and will refuse food.[6]

Children were removed from their mothers at the age of 3; thereafter, monthly visits were allowed. Some children were boarded out with foster families, but there was a tendency for the Poor Law authorities to send them to families living on 'out-relief' (the 'deserving poor' could sometimes receive relief payments without having to live in the workhouse). In these cases, the money the families received for fostering the children was deducted from their relief payments, and the parish made a saving.

Children were usually fostered with families outside their immediate district, and care was taken to sever any contact they might have had with their own relatives.

> The reason for this practice was to encourage relatives to accept orphan children voluntarily into their own families with no payments being involved, and thus to save the poor rate.[7]

We can see from this that kinship fostering was a common practice among the poor of England, and, although there was no legal adoption, a family would 'take in' its own rather than let relatives go to the workhouse.

This is still the case in some communities of working people, but there has never been any exact knowledge of its extent or the degree to which such fostering arrangements supplanted a child's connection with his own parents. There is a whole spectrum of possible arrangements, from a total transference of the parental function to mere baby-sitting while the mother goes out to work.

There were times when children were a valuable resource in the workhouse itself—as they grew up and could take on more of the domestic work of the place, the need for a large paid staff diminished. They were often used as unpaid labour in this way—just as the children in the Church's care grew up to fill its need for manpower.

More often, especially in times of economic depression, there were too many children in the workhouse. Apprenticeship was used as a means of fostering out the older ones. The choice of work for the children was limited by the fact that they usually received no training or education in the workhouse, but there were other factors to consider.

it is easy to see their origins in the Elizabethan Poor Law, for the choice of occupations was traditional and had changed little over the centuries. First, selected youngsters were directed to employment in local establishments to do work useful to the section of the community from which the Guardians were drawn. The clearest examples of this are domestic service and agricultural labour.[8]

To remove the children from the parish altogether, and avoid the risk of their coming back on the rates, there were even more drastic alternatives: the army, the navy, and the merchant marine. Emigration was a solution for both sexes: girls could go to the colonies as indentured domestic servants, contracted to work for an employer until they had paid off their fare. Boys were sent to dangerous jobs that no one else wanted to do— mining and fishing for example.

De facto adoption was known throughout this period, and this met with the consent of the Poor Law Guardians, if not exactly with their approval: 'English officials found it difficult to believe that there could be any relationship unless money was being paid for the child's keep.'[9]

The threat to this relationship might come from the authorities, but it was more likely to come from the child's family, who always had the legal right to claim him back. Foster parents who had grown attached to the child might pay blackmail money rather than surrender him.

None the less, the fact is that adoption was known to the English, and known by that name, at every period—even when it was not part of the law. Shakespeare has a description of it that is still exact:

> I say, I am your mother;
> And put you in the catalogue of those
> That were enwombed mine: 'tis often seen
> Adoption strives with nature, and choice breeds
> A native slip to us from foreign seeds;
> You ne'er oppress'd me with a mother's groan,
> Yet I express to you a mother's care.[10]

In spite of the widespread practice of adoption, there were many obstacles to the passage of an adoption law. To this day, most orphans are cared for by relatives, as are many children whose mothers must earn their living. The child whose parents cannot provide for it, whose mother is unmarried, or who through some other accident of fate comes into public care, has always been the 'adoptable' child. But when adoption was seen as one way of condoning immorality, and when just those people who could have encouraged it—the Church and the Poor Law authorities—did not do so, there was no pressure for it to achieve legal status. Add to this the fact that adoption interfered with the English law of inheritance, and the cards were heavily stacked against it.

Two major themes of Victorian fiction can be seen as bearing on the matter of adoption: the rescue of an orphan child, and the story of the changeling, or the child whose real parentage is suddenly and dramatically revealed. Along with these themes goes the overriding obsession with inheritance: the one accident, almost an act of God, that could suddenly change the social status of a person in a class-bound and very unequal society.

Some of these themes go right back to the Germanic fairy tales that were such favourites of the Victorians. 'Blue blood', surprise inheritance, and the revelation of concealed origins seem to be themes that are deeply embedded in the Anglo-Saxon psyche. From the frog who is changed into a prince to the denouement of *HMS Pinafore*, where the humble sailor and the captain are revealed to have been transferred in their cradles, the idea is the same.

It was also a favourite theme of Victorian children's literature. The works of Frances Hodgson Burnett offer many examples: the orphan drudge Sara Crewe, who turns out to be the ward of a rich colonial administrator, to the chagrin of the schoolmistress who has starved and exploited her, sets the tone for many such tales. The element of fantasy in such stories has been related by the psychoanalysts to the propensity for many children to invent idealized parentages for themselves—according to Freud, as a way of preserving the perfect images of the real parents, which have been tarnished by the revelation of their sexuality. These stories were aimed at children and appealed deeply to them; but adult fiction, too, was full of surprise inheritances and reversals of status.

The novels of George Eliot include the full spectrum of characters in early nineteenth-century England, and show very clearly the alternatives open to the unmarried mother, the orphan child, and others who were outside conventional society. Hetty in *Adam Bede* commits infanticide by exposing her child when her aristocratic lover refuses to marry her, and she is transported to the colonies in punishment. In a less realistic vein, the orphan child in *Silas Marner* is 'taken in' by the friendless old man: against all the expectations of modern child psychology, the little girl who spends her formative years tethered to the loom in the hut of the eccentric old weaver becomes a blossoming example of Christian young womanhood—but it turns out that there is a genuine Victorian explanation: her real father is an aristocrat, and 'blood tells'.

Many of the heroines in George Eliot's books are brought up by someone other than their real parents—in fact, relatives and other allies are lumped together in her parlance as 'friends'. Hetty is asked, when she goes to another district to bear her child, 'Where are your friends?'

Dickens' novels also contain many examples of fostering and *de facto* adoption. One of the most interesting is his portrait of

Tattycoram in *Little Dorrit*, a girl from the Coram Foundling Hospital who has been taken in by the Meagles family as a companion/servant to their own daughter. When Tattycoram rebels and seeks refuge with another embittered woman, Mr Meagles tries to win her back. The other woman says,

Here is your patron, your master. He is willing to take you back, my dear, if you are sensible of the favour and choose to go. You can be, again, a foil to his pretty daughter, a slave to her pleasant wilfulness, and a toy in the house showing the goodness of the family. You can have your droll name again, playfully pointing you out and setting you apart, as it is right that you should be pointed out and set apart. (Your birth, you know; you must not forget your birth.) You can again be shown to this gentleman's daughter, Harriet, and kept before her, as a living reminder of her own superiority and her gracious condescension.

This raises many of the issues that are still vexing adopters; and it shows why, for so long, genuine adoption was considered a moral and practical impossibility.

This was a society where the adoption of an heir made no difference to the descent of property; where money had largely taken the place of land, and more mouths to feed were a liability, not an asset. The countryside was becoming depopulated and enclosed; the crowded cities were sinks of unemployment. Concern was felt for the poor, and more especially for their children; but practical help was not forthcoming on a sufficient scale to avert the worst consequences of poverty.

We have concentrated on the poor because, as we have seen, the break-up of an indigent family was one of the few reasons for children to become available for fostering or adoption. Unlike more unified societies, where the exchange of children was part of the whole social transaction, there was nothing to induce a couple to part with a child at the behest of a childless relative.

In fact, separation from one's children was one of the worst consequences of the Poor Laws; even today in England, a family without a place to live may have to relinquish its children into care in order to qualify for a bed in a hostel. The punishment of poverty has still not come to an end.

64

We have seen that even in the Dark Ages, adoption did not die out completely in Europe. In England, the poor practised *de facto* adoption—often under pressure from the Poor Law authorities. The rich cared for orphaned relatives, and sometimes even rescued indigent children. There is no way of knowing the exact extent of these practices, but it is probably safe to say that the numbers involved increased from early Tudor times to the end of the nineteenth century, as industrialization affected more and more families and other systems of relief gradually disintegrated.

Thus although adoption was known in England, it was hampered by the absence of legal status. The countries with a heritage of Roman law continued to have adoption statutes on the books, even if they were not very often used. Adoption was sometimes resorted to by the aristocracy as a way of perpetuating itself; although, as a commentary on the French law points out, it had almost disappeared

> sous la double influence du christianisme et de la féodalite : pour l'Eglise Catholique, en effet, l'adoption n'était qu'une rivale du mariage qu'on ne pouvait donc favoriser et elle était contraire, en outre, au principe féodal de la conservation des biens dans les familles.
> [under the double influence of Christianity and feudalism : to the Catholic Church, in fact, adoption was nothing but a rival, and therefore less preferable, alternative to marriage. Besides, it was contrary to the feudal principle of retaining property within the family.][11]

The danger of extinction was always present to the aristocratic families, and some form of adoption continued to be an occasional necessity.

> Aristocratic lines on the point of becoming extinct were known to advertise for heirs, and it was thus that in 1864 M. Achille Lacroix was adopted by the last Vimeur de Rochambeau and became Lacroix de Vimeur de Rochambeau.[12]

But although it was the aristocracy who made most use of the archaic adoption laws that managed to survive, it was in fact the idea of democracy that paved the way for a revival of adoption as a popular institution. The importance of blood lines was challenged by the French revolutionaries:

> Au moment de la Révolution, l'adoption avait donc complètement disparu. L'état d'esprit qui caractérise l'époque révolutionnaire était favorable à la restauration de cette institution. En outre, la République Romaine et ses institutions avaient alors un grand prestige. Ceci explique que l'adoption ait été introduite dans la législation francaise par un décret du 18 janvier 1792 ...
> [At the time of the Revolution, adoption had almost completely disappeared. The attitudes that characterized the revolutionary era were favourable to the restoration of this institution. Besides, the Roman republic and its institutions were enjoying great prestige in this period. This explains why adoption was introduced into French law by a decree of 18 January 1792 ...][13]

The spread of democracy on the continent of Europe, and the revival of laws from the Roman Republic, did not reach as far as England, where the importance of blood ties, primogeniture, and inheritance through entail continued almost unabated. To bring about a revival of adoption required a more fluid social system, an underpopulated country, and a situation in which a man created his own place in the world and was not simply born into his rank.

These conditions obtained in the colonies of North America and the antipodes, most of which passed adoption laws seventy-five years before England. In their colonies, the French were more ready than the English to countenance the idea, which was after all part of their legal tradition. When Louisiana was a French possession, it had a Roman-based adoption law, which was in fact repealed when it became part of the United States.

The first modern adoption law in any part of the English-speaking world was the Massachusetts law of 1851. But *de facto* adoption had long been part of American practice, as European visitors were often surprised to discover.

Child welfare in the United States was based on English Poor Law ideas, and much of it was undertaken by religious groups. In this way some of the English obstacles to adoption were taken over to the New World, but they were overcome by the pioneer and farming families' self-sufficiency and need for manpower.

> Family life was subject to pioneer exigencies, In the first half of the eighteenth century two hundred fifty women and children taken by the Natchez, and retaken, were brought to New Orleans. The orphan girls were adopted by the Ursulines. The boys found homes in well-to-do families.[14]

The amazement of English visitors at how easily families absorbed indigent relatives, let alone totally unrelated children, shows how very unresponsive to this need the social structure of England had become. The visitors attributed the popularity of adoption to the abundance of food on a farm, but in fact the abundance was related to the amount of labour available: a situation no longer strictly true in manufacturing England. The increasing efficiency of machinery in factories and in agriculture meant that fewer hands were needed to produce the same amount. The United States still had vast tracts of wilderness to settle, and there were few substitutes for human labour on the frontier farms.

> Conditions facilitated adoption. 'One blessed custom they have in America,' wrote an English visitor in 1848, 'resulting from the abundance which they enjoy; a man dies, his widow and children are objects of peculiar care to the surviving branches of his family; the mother dies—her orphans find a home among her friends and relatives.' Another visitor in a work published in 1852 said: 'Observing how easily and frankly children are adopted in the United States, how pleasantly the scheme goes on, and how little of the wormwood of domestic jealousies, or the fretting prickle of neighbors' criticisms seem to interfere with it, one is led to enquire why the benevolent practice is so common there ... The facility with which enough, and more than enough, is found to satisfy every hungry mouth on a farm, gives wonderful scope to the benevolent sentiment ... A fresh hand growing up is valuable to the sons of

labor, who are quite as ready to adopt a child as the wealthy.'[15]

The scheme did not always go on so easily and pleasantly on the farms of frontier America. The Children's Aid Society, one of the first home-finding organizations for homeless children, was founded by Dr Loring Brace, 'who conceived the dubious idea of picking up homeless children from New York's Lower East Side and shipping them west in boxcars to be picked out by waiting farmers and their wives as farm and kitchen help.'[16]

Adoption was for long only a variant on the traditional Poor Law system of lodging indigent children in exchange for their labour. When it became more than that, and the passage of laws attempted to ensure that adopted children were well-treated, the whole process still faced a great deal of opposition. Most of this was of a class nature: adopted children were likely to be of a social origin quite different from that of the adopters, who, as a result, tended to expect the kind of behaviour they attributed to the local lower class.

The Reverend Martin T. Lamb, the founder of the New Jersey Children's Home Society, observed that: 'Very few families ... were willing to adopt a child if he was born and raised in their neighborhood, especially if he was a product of the almshouse.'[17]

The Protestant sects founded the early adoption societies in the United States—their notions of Christian charity involved them in many kinds of social work, and they were not committed, as the Catholics were, to the idea that the religious life involved seceding from the secular world.

There were celibate Protestant communities, like the Shakers, that perpetuated themselves through adoption—this was often done by arrangement with the local government, which placed children with communities willing to take them in order to save the cost of their support. By and large, however, the Protestant churches had no monastic establishment that was in any way a rival of the family, and although they ran institutions for homeless children, they were receptive to the idea of foster placement and adoption.

The state itself was much slower to recognize the benefits it could derive from the practice of adoption. Opposition came from several sources: the moralists continued to think that adoption enabled unmarried mothers to 'get away with it' and avoid the lasting stigma and punishment of having to raise their own children. The belief that adopting families only wanted the children in order to exploit them was slow to die. Above all, the provision of comprehensive social services, including adoption, seemed unjustifiably expensive—especially when the Church social work agencies were willing to do it themselves.

The religious monopoly of adoption in the United States has been so tenacious that a recent (1965) strategic guide to potential adopters could say that: 'The couple who is not affiliated with a church and does not want to become affiliated or even wish to pretend to be affiliated may have to abandon hope of adopting through an agency.'[18]

Even in the relatively fluid societies produced by colonialism, there were great differences in the definition of the ruling group and who could be admitted to it. Unfortunate members of this group, such as orphans, could be re-incorporated into it by means of adoption, and illegitimate members of it could be legitimated or adopted. The propensity of the ruling group to take care of its own was given a push by the need to distinguish itself from other castes: in the United States, these included Indians, blacks, Catholics and Jews, and foreigners of all kinds.

Since, in England, the other social groups had been racially indistinguishable from the ruling class, the extension to them of social welfare measures met opposition. This heritage produced similar results in the United States, but the out-groups were differently (usually racially) defined. The Catholic colonists treated the whole problem differently—the illegitimate sons of the rulers could be admitted to the ruling caste, no matter what their race. Adoption as such was unnecessary, and to this day many South American countries have no adoption law. Edmund Leach sees this as a basic structural difference between Catholicism and Protestantism—the role of Mary as the concubine of God, and God's acceptance of Jesus as his son, creates a social precedent for Catholics to follow.

The Christian myth is compatible with a social system that is essentially patriarchal, in which it is taken for granted that the rulers are so vastly superior to the ruled that class difference almost ossifies into caste, a society in which the lords never marry into the lower classes, but in which they will graciously deign to take slave concubines and elevate their sons to the ranks of the elite. Such societies have in fact repeatedly emerged in Christendom, notably in Byzantium and eighteenth-century Brazil, both countries where the cult of the Virgin was exceptionally well developed.[19]

Although adoption early became law in the United States it was only practised by the white ruling group—and the agencies were only created by, and intended to serve, this group. Other castes may have practised *de facto* adoption on a much wider scale, as a means of family survival in times of poverty and dislocation, but they did it without benefit of law.

The English problem was that once adoption became law, confusion might arise in the class system. The punishing of poverty might have to stop; the poor might begin to use the alleviating mechanisms intended for their betters.

Much has been made of the awakening of the social conscience of the West at the end of the nineteenth century; but in fact society came to consider poverty unacceptable not because of its affront to the liberal sensibility (it took a deliberate excursion to the East End of London even to come into contact with real poverty), but because of its affront to the economy and the national strength. The recruits for the Boer War were so malnourished and under-educated that almost half of them were considered unfit for military service; and the standards of the army were none too high. It was this kind of realization that awoke the 'conscience of the nation'.

The private charities in England followed roughly the example of the public agencies in their means tests and criteria of 'deservingness'. But they were more willing to apply modern methods in their efforts to solve the problems they dealt with, and there were many new ideas about that promised to work better than the workhouse.

Nigel Middleton observed, in *When Family Failed*, that: 'Much of the modern history of social welfare is concerned with the resistance of the Poor Law-based system to the introduction of liberal measures influenced by modern psychology.'[20] Modern psychology had a friend at court in the form of the growing realization that fostering cost the state less than keeping children in institutions; and that adoption, after the formalities were completed, cost nothing at all. Foster parents were suspect for many years simply because they were paid: there was an abiding suspicion that they were doing it only for money, and periodic scandals about the 'baby-farming' methods of private fostering added to public mistrust. But fostering, either by relatives, neighbours, or paid baby-sitters, was established practice among the industrial poor of the cities, in which both parents had to earn a wage to support the family. This added to its shady reputation among the middle classes.

But the childless middle-class woman now wanted to adopt. Her domestic role had shrunk until it consisted of little more than the care of young children, and if she was deprived of this function, she felt herself to be useless indeed. Stories of such women 'taking in' a working-class or illegitimate baby and then being blackmailed by the natural parents, who of course still had the legal right to claim it back, added to pressure for the passing of an Adoption Act.

It was recognized even at the time that adoption would become part of the classic English pattern of self-perpetuating elites: it would serve the well-off families who chose to use it, without necessarily rescuing all the indigent children who were available for adoption.

> It was usual (in the 16th and 17th centuries) for the more substantial citizens to take into their household the sons and daughters of the less wealthy on a variety of contracts, ranging from page, through apprentice to child labourer. Consequently, the richer households tended to be large, while the poor ones consisted of parents and the younger children only.[21]

Similar patterns in China and Japan merged into the widespread practice of adoption. As the various client groups of European families decreased in number and size, there were few roles the child of another family could play. The only appropriate status open to him, in many cases, was that of adopted child.

Obstacles to adoption gradually diminished. The feudal

system of land-holding became less significant as property was converted into money. The Poor Law system of relief, when faced with the vast slums created by industrialism, became increasingly unworkable.

During the rise of the British Empire, the English came to see themselves as a precious few surrounded by hostile tribes; in this situation, home-grown slum children were acceptable as never before. Attributing undesirable traits to genes rather than to social deprivation is a widespread habit of mind—as we will see, the controversy over the innate intelligence of black people is one of the vexed issues in American adoption today. But this problem can be seen in perspective when we note that every proletarian class was popularly supposed to be stupider, less moral, and less trustworthy than its superiors; and that the 'stupid' class in one country may become the masters in another, and thus begin to attribute stupidity to someone else.

This is what happened to the English in the nineteenth and early twentieth centuries. English plebeians were now the rulers in America, Australia, and South Africa; any Englishman could claim superiority to the 'natives' ruled by the mother country.

But it was the First World War that finally pushed England into legislating. The war orphans made a more sentimental appeal to the conscience than did the waifs of the 'undeserving poor' or the bastards of 'immoral' women. But when the middle classes showed themselves willing to take in the victims of the fighting in poor, defenceless little Belgium, the charitable workers pointed out that while Belgium wanted to keep its own children, there were many to be had right in the heart of England. Interest in overseas adoption thus stimulated interest in the adoption of available children in England itself—a pattern that has been repeated with inter-country and inter-racial adoption in more recent years.

Adoption after the First World War had a patriotic tinge: often the goal was to replace a child killed in the war, or for a widow to find a new interest in life. Class matching was also a feature of agency work in this period, and class solidarity in the face of social change was another impetus to adoption. It was closely related to other forms of charity, as can be seen in the 1921–22 report of the National Children Adoption Association:

We have also been able to help in finding people willing to educate boys of gentle birth whose parents are too poor to send them to a private or public school; in some cases this has been done as a war-memorial for a beloved son who fell in the war ...

If charity was one motive for adoption, adopters still hoped for a result satisfactory to themselves, and it was the self-imposed duty of the agencies to be stringent in selecting the children they placed. In 1929–30, the National Children Adoption Association arranged 255 adoptions—and turned away 550 children from its baby nursery. Although matching was the aim, the fact was that poor people gave up their babies and people who could afford to do so adopted. Thus the 1930–31 report could say: 'The great majority of those confided to our care find adopters whose circumstances are better than those of their own parents.'

In the years before the First World War, there were at any one time perhaps 80,000 children dependent on Poor Law residential care. The cycle of deprivation was in full operation: the products of the institution were drawn into prostitution, crime, illegitimacy, and their children too were eventually taken into care.

It has been said that the great institutions founded to rescue these children—Dr Barnardo's, Coram's, the 'Waifs and Strays' which became the Church of England Children's Society— were better places in the past than such institutions are today. The children and staff were permanent residents; today's pattern of children going in and out of care, and staff being replaced every few months, was then unknown. Moreover, the children were instructed that they were privileged to be there.

Perhaps there was a measure of social stability in these places; but the personality they produced was universally seen as unlovable, uncooperative, and all but unemployable. The success stories are few; they are balanced by statistics like the mortality rate (50 per cent annually in some London children's homes in the mid-nineteenth century).

In spite of all these reasons for the necessity of legal adoption, Parliament was remarkably reluctant to legislate. Not personally concerned with children in need, most of the legislators feared the effect of adoption on the country's morality and on the laws of inheritance.

The debate in the House of Commons neatly encapsulated many of the issues that are still being argued over in connection with adoption; it also typified the debates held in other legislatures, in other Western countries, when they came to face the same problem. The political implications of adoption legislation were brought out more clearly than at any time before or since.

The barriers of conventional morality and inheritance were so strong that even after a favourable report by a Parliamentary committee, the question had to be presented in the guise of patriotism. Six Private Members' Bills were introduced, and failed, before the 1926 session that saw the success of the measure. That session began with the omission of adoption from the King's speech, to the chagrin of the M.P.s who had worked for its inclusion.

> a promise was made in this House by the Prime Minister that there would be proposals introduced for the legalising of adoption. Last Session it was pointed out that, particularly since the War, a great many children whose parents had been killed in the War and who had been left destitute, had been adopted and were without any proper legal status. A Committee had been sitting under Mr Justice Tomlin, which made a report recommending that the English law be brought into line with the law of practically every other country in the world and allow legalised adoption. That was not the crack-brained idea of a Socialist, but the recommendation of a Judge of the High Court ... [22]

The Socialists got their own back during the debate at the second reading of the Bill, which had bi-partisan support.

> I want to support the Bill, because, in the first place, I want to take the opportunity of saying that the party with which I am associated are not guilty of the charges that have been so frequently made against us at election times, that we want to nationalise women and children and put them all into institutions.[23]

74

Clement Attlee brought out the fact that adoption was of serious interest to the Labour Party, because it touched on the lives of their constituents.

> We have had a good deal of reference to property and the idea of childless couples adopting children, but what we find in East London is that, where some misfortune befalls a family, there is nothing so common as the adoption of the children by neighbours—adoption frequently by a couple who already, one would think, had quite a heavy enough burden in looking after their own children.[24]

It was also indicated that there were other reasons for Parliamentary interest in adoption:

> In some countries where they have had a system of adoption in force for some time, I am told that it is a very fruitful source of litigation. Whether that is an evil depends of course on the point of view from which you look at it. Speaking as a practising member of the Bar I cherish my own views.[25]

All in all, it was necessary to legislate for the soundest of reasons: 'We must realize that adoption *de facto* is taking place all the time and that it is right that what is *de facto* should be made *de jure*, so that people may know precisely where they are.'[26]

When it came to details, many things were debated that have not been solved to this day. The question of secrecy was seen to involve several paradoxes. If adoption were secret, and the identity of natural parents and adopters unknown to each other, how could incest (which would be illegal in both families) be avoided? More pertinent still, how could the adopted child inherit on the intestacy of his natural parent, a right it was decided he should still have, if he and the parent lost sight of each other's whereabouts? This is still puzzling: the adoptees in the United States today, who are pressing for their civil right to know their original identity, were advised at 4th N.A.C.A.C. that if they presented their case in this light, no court in the land would decide against them.

75

The proponents of secrecy pointed out that because most adopted children were illegitimate, they should have their origins buried in their own interests. To be adopted would brand them in the public mind as illegitimate, even after the technical change of status brought about by adoption. But even this point of view was challenged on the grounds that it made adoption itself seem shameful: 'In the public mind there ought to be a feeling that it is a perfectly honourable relationship between the child and the adopted parents.'[27]

One of the proposed (but unsuccessful) amendments was that adoption should be made revocable in case it turned out badly; the notorious case was mentioned of a 'vegetarian itinerant secularist lecturer' who was raising three adopted boys 'on grape nuts and without the Bible'.

Catholics sought in vain an amendment to prevent children going to adopters of a different religion from that of their natural parents; this failed on the ground that 'In these matters we have, first of all, to consider the welfare of the infants. I am not for a moment suggesting that the question of religious belief is not a most important thing, but it is not the only thing ...'[28] The same argument has been used in recent years to justify adoption across racial and national lines.

Even after the law was passed, its implementation depended to a large extent on agency practice. And the agencies showed the influence of Poor Law legislation that made the unwed mother a criminal. Until the passing of the Adoption Act, the mother could be imprisoned in the workhouse for two years as the price of having the child taken off her hands by the authorities—and when the Church of England and the local councils began opening shelters for unmarried mothers, they often exchanged care and lodging for two years' unpaid labour. A private agency could charge about £60 for arranging an adoption, and even after the Act was passed, things were not much better:

After 1926, it was openly agreed by those working in the field that the demand for children exceeded the supply, thus allowing for a double rake-off, the first payment coming from the girl for being relieved of her child, the second for finding a suitable child from couples who were willing to pay sums ranging from £5 to £100.[29]

The adoption of infants at this time was the exception rather than the rule; adopters often wanted a child past the nappy stage, to make things easier for themselves; and some wanted even older children, and were suspected of using them as cheap domestic labour. Perhaps the relatively advanced age of adopted children contributed to the widespread feeling that the outcome of adoption was extremely dubious. The careful preparation that today paves the way for such an adoption was then unknown; and expecting gratitude from a child with an early history in one of the children's homes of the day was almost guaranteed to produce the opposite result.

Ironically, the English law, when it finally arrived, benefited from its newness. There were no precedents to hamper the legislators, and they were able to incorporate the ideas about adoption that seemed most relevant, not those that were part of an archaic legal tradition.

In France, the post-Revolutionary idea that adoption should be total in its effects and open to everyone was drastically modified in the Civil Code of 1902—the more rigid aspects of the Roman inheritance were again given precedence in law. The adopter had to be at least 50 years old and without legitimate heirs; the adoptee must have reached his majority. The connection between inheritance and adoption was re-established in these laws.

The English and American laws, by contrast, always concerned themselves with the creation of a new family—in many cases only minors could be adopted. The adopters had to be adults, but it was unimportant whether or not they were past child-bearing age: the reason for the advanced age demanded in the Roman-based laws. In fact, although the Anglo-Saxon laws did not stipulate an upper age-limit, it quickly became agency practice to seek adopters who might plausibly have borne the child they adopted.

English adoption law, because it was first promulgated for children already in the care of the state, always involved the state as an intermediary. Ancient adoption law was a contract between two parties, legalized before a judge. But in England, it was a transaction between the child's previous caretaker — the state — and the adopters. Thus the 'guardian *ad litem*', 'next friend', and other representatives of the 'best interest of the child' were mentioned in the laws. Such a representative is meant to be disinterested: that is, he cannot be one of the people actually arranging the adoption. Their role was to investigate the adopters and give them the child if they were found satisfactory. This made it easier to provide adoption services as part of the state's total social welfare effort: officialdom was already on the scene.

The English and colonial laws were expressly formulated to deal with a new situation: the break-up of extended families in the industrial cities. It was better suited to solving these problems than was the cumbrous Roman law. Thus the provisions of English law began to have an impact everywhere in the world — a process that was hastened by colonialism.

4 The West Today

In adoption as in so many other areas, the cultural and legal norm of the non-communist world is coming to be that of the Anglo-Saxon countries. The wide variety of attitudes and practices once found throughout the world is gradually becoming standardized—and this standardization is reflected in Geneva conventions, Hague conventions, international concords of all kinds.

There are obvious advantages to this in a mobile society. Disputes about the legal status of a child adopted in another country can be sorted out; an adopted child can be assured of his inheritance; adoptive parents do not risk losing the child. Uniformity ensures that adoption is understood by everyone in the same way.

The main influence of Anglo-Saxon adoption law stems from its intolerance of any kind of semi-adopted status. If adoption is to exist at all in a society where possession, ownership, and materialism hold sway it must be made absolutely total and watertight. This has been the nature of the laws in England and the United States, and their colonies throughout this century. Inheritance from the natural family has gradually been replaced by inheritance from the adopters, and the obligation to support the natural parents, where it existed, has largely been done away with.

The impetus behind many of these changes has been that the only way parental rights could be transferred was through adoption. Either the adopters became the parents, and thus had total legal jurisdiction over the child, or they did not, and the natural parents could claim it. Foster parents who did not adopt had no ultimate rights over the child at all, regardless of the length of its stay with them, except in extreme cases where the court had terminated the rights of the natural parents because of neglect or abuse.

This all-or-nothing system is, as we shall see, under attack from many quarters today. It is blamed for keeping children in the care of the state and preventing their adoption; for the removal of children from foster homes to which they had grown attached; and for creating the necessity for adoption in situations such as fostering by relatives where it might be inappropriate.

The sharing of parental rights, rather than their total investment in one set of parents, is an idea much talked about today. But at a time when the family itself seems to be disintegrating, rather than assimilating new members, what sort of group is going to share these rights and obligations? The kibbutz, the commune, the 'group home' —these are some of the suggestions that have been put forward. But all of them so far have suffered from the fact that they are running counter to the prevailing trend, which is for the family group to become ever smaller and thus more intensely bound together.

As the West is searching for solutions to the problems of the increasingly dominant but increasingly unpopular nuclear family, other areas are discovering 'western' adoption for the first time. The bastions of the Arab world and the Mediterranean are beginning to fall; parts of Asia and Africa are moving towards a 'metropolitan' system. In part, this is because the spread of Western-style 'development' creates Western-style social problems, the fruit of urbanization and dislocation, and necessitates Western solutions like non-relative adoption. In part, too, it is because the assumption of Western customs is seen by many poor countries as the path to economic development.

The Soviet Union and the Eastern European countries, as well as Israel, have experimented with communal solutions to social problems. But they, too, seem to be currently defining the nuclear family as the domestic ideal, and using adoption as one way to make it work for everyone.

But there is another trend, of great interest to Western theoreticians who are trying to see where we can go from here. In countries with a strong tradition of adoption or kinship fostering, where the extended family has been incorporated into a modern social pattern, the advent of socialism or communism seems to be building on what was there before without the kind

80

of discontinuity the capitalist nations have suffered. Decentralization, self-sufficiency, and balanced, local development are the keys to the strength of China, North Vietnam, and Tanzania, as they were to the Chinese family and the African village.

Is it possible to apply this kind of model successfully in the industrial, centralized Western countries? Black Americans are trying to do it in their own communities; Cuba has seceded from the Western metropolis and is trying to define its own development in these terms. But it is still too early to tell what will be the outcome of these trends, as it is too early to predict what will happen to the over-extended, over-developed capitalist world order.

When we look in detail at what is happening to various countries today, we can see how the spread of economic development is swiftly followed by the problems of children in care, family breakdown, and growing popularity of adoption. We will also see how a child-exporting country becomes a child-importing country at a certain stage in its evolution; and how adoption 'follows the flag' in imperialist wars.

In Europe, modern adoption laws have usually been grafted on to existing laws, with results that often make adoption more difficult than the legislators intended it to be. Not every country is willing to jettison such legal traditions as the obligation of children and parents to support each other; or the right of natural parents to know the identity of the adopters and to keep up relations with the child.

We have seen that under Roman law, adoption only took place in the absence of natural children, and when the parents were above the age when they could expect to have any. This is the tradition that most of the European countries have had to contend with in framing their present adoption laws, and movement away from it has been slow. The International Union for Child Welfare places it at the head of its list of motives that offer resistance to the idea of adoption:

—the survival of Roman law
—pseudo-religious morals
—family and social convention
—erroneous ideas about blood ties
—fear of heredity

—fear of the mother's return and fear of scandal

—and, above all, losing sight of the priority interests involved, that is to say the interests of the child, which are all too often sacrificed to a number of interests of secondary importance.[1]

The European Convention on the Adoption of Children, completed in April 1967, has attempted to influence member countries of the Council of Europe to modernize their adoption laws. So far, the Convention has only been ratified by Ireland, Malta, Norway, Sweden, Switzerland, and the U.K., but its influence can be seen in recent legal changes in a number of other countries.

The Convention provides that:

Adoption confers on the adopted person in respect of the adopter the rights and obligations of every kind that a child born in lawful wedlock has in respect of his father or mother.
The number of children who may be adopted by an adopter shall not be restricted by law. A person who has, or is able to have, a child born in lawful wedlock, shall not on that account be prohibited by law from adopting a child. If adoption improves the legal position of a child, a person shall not be prohibited by law from adopting his own child not born in lawful wedlock.

In most of the European countries, there is a desperate shortage of babies to adopt, combined with a crisis in the numbers of children being cared for by the state. This paradoxical situation has a number of causes, only some of which are related to the adoption laws. But increasing efforts are being made to see how adoption can be used to solve both situations at once, and some of these efforts involve trying to cut through the jungle of law and red tape that has grown up around European adoption.

There is another element in the European situation that has given rise to the most explosive controversy of all. This is abortion. Whether it should be legalized in places where there are still couples waiting to adopt; whether girls seeking abor-

82

tions are being pressured (or even paid) to have their babies and give them up for adoption; which of the two alternatives has the most severe effect on the mental health of the mother — these are the questions that most European countries are now debating.

Although the two are so often viewed as alternatives, the fact is that abortion and adoption have the same friends. Campaigns to legalize the one coincide with campaigns to facilitate the other. Both seem to their proponents to involve the same issues: basically, the right of individuals to choose their fate, and to create their families when and how they wish. Doctors who refuse abortions, and governments that make them illegal, are viewed in the same light as social agencies that place obstacles in the way of adoption. It is the 'client' groups—adoptive parents and women who have had abortions—who in both cases are leading the movement for change.

We can see the various stages in the movement for change as we move northwards through Europe. The Mediterranean countries are just beginning the debate; in Italy, for example, it is now said that the battle of divorce is won: that of abortion is about to begin. France, Switzerland and Germany form another group, where the principles of individual choice are widely accepted but still face legal barriers. In England and Scandinavia, the debate has entered another stage—the movement towards adoption and abortion is largely completed, and new doubts are arising about the universal applicability — and exportability—of these solutions.

The Mediterranean family has remained more close-knit than that of the northern European countries. The fostering of related children, the role of grandparents, the legal situation of women, who are first under the protection of their fathers and then of their husbands—such elements of tradition have meant that adoption played a peripheral role and was rarely used when there was any other method available of caring for a child.

The strong desire for children in these societies has never been filled by adoption, which has until recently been legally restricted to those over 50. The woman seeking to fulfil her customary role has no recourse if she is childless, and this can be seen in full force as recently as the early 1940s, when Lorca's

Yerma was written. 'Every woman has blood for four or five sons, and if she does not bear them, it turns to poison.'

The Roman-based adoption laws, which could not come into effect until the middle age of the parents and the majority of the child, could do little to help the childless woman, whose feelings of worth and position in the family were undermined by her condition. Nor could it help the child without a family, since he could not be adopted fully until he grew up.

Spain, Portugal and Italy are the countries where the force of Roman law is still the strongest. All three still maintain the Roman distinction between 'full' and 'less full' adoption. So strong is this tradition that even though Portugal had no adoption law at all until 1967, it incorporated the two-tier system into its new law. In all these countries, however, 'less full' adoption may eventually become full adoption, so that it is possible to achieve a certain measure of security by adopting a child under the former law and then, when such requirements as the age and length of marriage of the adopters have been fulfilled, to complete the formalities.

Limited adoption in Portugal is reversible 'for reasons of succession rights'—by this means the adopted child can be disinherited if the parents have their own natural child after adopting; or if the adopted child's natural parents are likely to die without an heir, they can reclaim the child.

In Spain, the rights of the natural parents are protected even more stringently. The only adoptable children are foundlings or abandoned children who have not been claimed within three years. The adoptee must consent to his own adoption if he is of age; otherwise, 'those who would be required to consent to his marriage must give their consent'—another parallel between marriage and adoption. The adoption is irrevocable, and the adoptee inherits from his new family in full: undoubtedly one reason why adoption is made so difficult.

These laws have a long history, but like the traditional position of women, they are under attack in the Mediterranean countries. Italy may try to revoke its new divorce law, and Austria may continue to be the only Catholic country with legalized abortion, but there is little doubt that in the next few years the adoption laws will show signs of change.

The Spanish press attacked the British adoption law several years ago for deciding that the English adoptive parents of a Spanish baby could keep the child, even though the provisions of Spanish adoption law had not been fulfilled. But the resulting uproar led to public examination of the Spanish law, and the consensus was that with so many children in orphanages, it was unfortunate that the law barred those with their own children from adopting.

In Italy, the legal situation is similar. The Church has over the centuries paid little attention to adoption, confining its rulings to the degrees of prohibited marriage for an adopted child—that is, whether the incest provisions of canon law apply in cases of adoption, and whether they only apply in full adoption.

The child-care institutions of Italy have recently been under attack again. The 1970 scandal of children being beaten and starved in an institution run by nuns has many less dramatic parallels that have not hit the international headlines. Today there are perhaps 40,000 institutions in Italy caring for almost 300,000 orphaned or abandoned children (compared with about 20,000 such children in Britain). The migration of southerners to the industrial cities of the north has caused much of the problem of family break-up; so has the unequal distribution of wealth in a country where economic growth has only benefited certain sectors of the population.

The proliferation of agencies, and of people to staff them, is a bureaucratic nightmare—and since many of the staff are political appointees and patronage jobs, no one wants to begin the task of rationalization. Little of the 1,000 million lire a year that passes through the hands of these institutions is actually used for the children in their care.

The plight of the children has reached the proportions of a national scandal. A White Paper prepared by Communist M.P.s who are attempting to bring about reforms says that in the decade 1958–68, the number of abandoned children in northern Italy dropped by 8·5 per cent, while in the south it rose by 31 per cent. Groups 'peripheral' to the economy, migrating in search of work, are forced into a situation where even an inadequate institution is more likely to be able to provide for its children than the family itself.

Headlines have been made in recent years by the sale of children to nunneries, mistreatment and corruption in both Church and secular institutions, and mismanagement of funds — in the Rome Chapter of Onmi, the Christian Democrat child welfare agency, only a third of the 1,216,000 lire a year it receives for its homeless children reaches the children themselves.

A recent report in the *Guardian* unearthed a sampling of facts from this confused nightmare:

> One institute exists for the care of 'working-class orphans, so that they be brought up, educated, and instructed in the ways proper to the class to which they belong'.
>
> A home in Brescia will admit only children who are 'of sound constitution, vaccinated, not deficient, and of the Aryan race'. Near Brindisi, in the Villa Nazareth of Ostuni, there are 80 misfits in that institute of correction. They range in age from five to nine.[2]

The Italian adoptive parents' organization recognizes that adoption will not by itself solve such a gigantic problem. Many, if not most, of the children in institutions have families who are unable to care for them. The court mechanism to review all the cases, decide on availability for adoption, and do the placement work is hampered by lack of staff. Thus the president of the organization says:

> Those who in the last few years have promoted above all the adoption side of the picture have realized that it is more urgent and more necessary to work for the elimination of the causes of abandonment and institutionalization by actively promoting the establishment of community social welfare services, of direct assistance for the family of origin in need, of group foster homes within the community etc.[3]

Estimates for the number of children in care in France approach those for Italy — 200,000 at any one time, and possibly 100,000 more in private fostering arrangements.

Trois cent mille enfants n'ont plus de foyer. 100,000 couples sont prêts à les accueillir. Mais 4,500 orphelins seulement sont 'adoptables'. Voila, en trois chiffres secs, tout le drame de l'adoption en France ...
[300,000 children have no homes. 100,000 couples are ready to welcome them. But a mere 4,500 orphans are 'adoptable'. There, in three stark figures, you have the whole drama of adoption in France ...][4]

To this must be added another number: an estimated 800,000 illegal abortions a year, half the number of live births. The abortion debate has been raging more hotly in France than anywhere else, and although the passage of a new Abortion Bill has temporarily calmed the storm, opposition to the measure has by no means died away. Adoption is still being used as one source of ammunition for both sides.

It seems to some legislators and parents' groups to be a simple matter to divert a few pregnant women from the abortionist to the adoption society. It is pointed out that on the 'underground railway' to the London abortion clinics, many girls are persuaded by unscrupulous doctors to have their babies and relinquish them for a profit; that, in France itself, there is a clandestine traffic in babies; and that the psychological consequences of giving up a baby for adoption need not be any worse than those of an abortion.

However, the women themselves do not accept these arguments. Whether or not the women of France are in favour of legalized abortion—and the polls now show that the majority are—they are voting by their actions for abortion rather than adoption. They are in no doubt, it seems, about which set of psychological consequences they would prefer. The number of illegal abortions in France showed the same drastic changes in the late 1960s as in England and the United States. In the latter countries, new laws were thought to be the cause of the sudden increase in abortions; the French example shows that it would have happened anyway. The law has simply followed an irresistible trend, and made *de jure* what was *de facto*. This movement reached France in 1974, when a Bill liberalizing abortion was finally passed.

Whether the rise in abortions is the real cause of the baby

shortage has also been an area of controversy in France. The numbers of children in care, which still far outweigh the numbers of applications to adopt, indicate that other solutions are possible. Indeed this is the view of most of the groups of adoptive parents and of the government itself, who are all concentrating their efforts on streamlining the judicial procedures surrounding adoption and ensuring that someone is responsible for finding homes for children who need them. The debate on abortion in the French legislature explicitly concluded that abortion was not responsible for the shortage of adoptable babies—that bureaucratic delay and obstructive laws were the culprits. The Minister of Justice said he would not like to see the two questions linked, as it then became a matter of poor women bearing babies for the homes of the better-off.

The anti-abortion lobby is the most explicit in connecting adoption to abortion. They say that adoption is the only honest solution for an unwanted pregnancy, and that one must 'déculpabiliser l'abandon en le transformant en un geste d'amour socialement efficace.' ['remove the guilt from abandonment and transform it into a socially useful gesture of love.'] The adoptive parents' organizations are reluctant to use this argument, saying that 'la lutte contre l'avortement n'est pas non plus une "solution honnête" aux problèmes de l'adoption.' ['The anti-abortion struggle is not an "honest solution" to the problems of adoption either.']

'Déculpabiliser l'abandon' is viewed by almost everyone, however, as a means of making more children available for adoption. Some believe that changes in terminology are all-important—that if neutral terms like 'consent to adoption' or 'transfer of parental rights' were used, more parents would be willing to allow the children they cannot care for themselves to be adopted.

But terminology is not the only thing that will have to be changed in a country where, as Le Monde reports (December 14th, 1973), fewer than 2 per cent of young mothers could envision placing their children for adoption if they were unable to care for them. The need for adoption has outstripped its acceptance; and even where adoption itself is acceptable, the relinquishment of a child is widely considered unthinkable. There is no reason to suppose that the accident of an unwanted pregnancy immediately induces a woman to stop sharing this attitude.

This is one reason why, although the number of babies 'abandoned' to the care of the state has decreased sharply, the number of older children coming into care has continued to increase. Only the difficulties of caring for a child will induce the mother to part with it: before she has experienced these difficulties, she cannot countenance the idea.

The French courts reflect this conservatism. Recent judicial decisions include one that the parents of four children in care should not be declared to have abandoned them, although the children had not seen them for eight years; that a couple called Trognon [stump] could not adopt because they had a 'ridiculous' surname; and in general that the rights of parents who declare their intention to reclaim their children cannot be terminated.

The rights of parents still take precedence over the rights of children in many ways, not least in the law that forbids adoption to a family with legitimate children. Michel Poniatowski, the Minister of Public Health, stated in an interview that 'l'objectif de l'adoption est de rendre heureux le plus grand nombre d'enfants et, dans la mesure du possible, le plus grand nombre de parents.' ['The objective of adoption is to make the greatest number of children happy and, insofar as possible, the greatest number of parents.']⁵ He declared his intention of creating a national office of adoptions, to debate changes in law and procedure and eventually to function as a resource exchange among the departments of France. The new minister of health, Simone Weil, is now putting this idea into effect.

Perhaps the major obstacle to adoption in France, according to many observers, is the attitude of the social services and agencies. *Le Monde* notes (December 14th, 1973) that the provision in the 1966 adoption law for the renunciation of parental rights in favour of the Aide Sociale à l'Enfance (the state agency) is open to abuse, but that, nevertheless, the agency has usually been reproached for not making enough use of its powers, for devoting too much attention to studying infants to ensure their perfection before placement, and for not cutting through legal red tape. The Aide Sociale, it says, wishes only to place children 'plus beaux et plus sains que les enfants légitimes' ['more beautiful and healthier than legitimate children'].

One woman who finally adopted in Switzerland, having waited several years in France, said 'It's scandalous that the authorities in France do not facilitate adoption. There are enough babies to satisfy all the requests.' Even after the year of abandonment required for judicial termination of parental rights, first the social agency and then the court make attempts to locate the natural mother and ask her wishes—a process that may take several years. Some of the French parents' organizations believe that the period of abandonment should be shortened to six months; all believe that the judicial inquiry is unnecessarily long and repetitive.

The agencies usually consider a child to be unadoptable once it has reached the age of 6. Not only do the lengthy adoption procedures mean that this often happens before a child can be placed, but the children coming into care are already older than they used to be. The number of children placed over the age of 3 jumped 15 per cent between 1961 and 1967, and 40 per cent in 1970 alone. Forty-eight per cent of the infants received by the state agency are born of foreign parents, immigrant workers for the most part (another instance of the social disabilities suffered by a peripheral economic group).

The mixed blood of many of these children is another reason why the agencies consider them only marginally adoptable, although many parents are willing to adopt them. According to *France-Soir* (December 19th, 1973): 'En général les couples commencent par demander un bébé de race blanche, puis, devant les difficultés, ils décident de le prendre de couleur.' ['In general, couples begin by asking for a white baby; then, faced with all the difficulties, they decide to take a coloured one.']

The French insistence that adopters be middle-class is also very strong. The latest statistics from the Aide Sociale à l'Enfance list the professions of 172 adopters:

52 cadres du secteur privé [businessmen]
28 employés [salaried employees]
27 fonctionnaires [civil servants]
23 professions libérales [professionals]

20 ouvriers [workers]
16 commercants [tradesmen]
6 industriels [industrialists]

There is a thriving black market in France, and an even more thriving 'grey market'. Couples can even find babies by placing advertisements in the press, offering to pay the expenses of the birth and to give the baby a comfortable home. It is not an illegal procedure, if no money changes hands and if no intermediary profits from the transaction. The adoption of a child under 2 years of age must be done through an agency, but if the adoptive family waits until they have had the child for two years, they can complete the formalities with no agency involvement. The minimum age for adopters is 30 in France, but French agencies, like English ones, do not like to place babies with couples too old to be their natural parents. Thus the years spent on waiting lists mean that many parents are too old to adopt by the time their chance comes.

The French are also turning to another means of alleviating infertility—donor insemination. Perhaps a thousand babies a year are now born in France by this means, in spite of official Catholic and Jewish opposition to what they call 'mechanical adultery' which introduces a third party into the conjugal relationship. The donor and his wife must sign away parental rights in the infant, and the husband of the mother must sign a statement freeing her from accusations of adultery.

In France, adoption has a great deal of Government support: the idea that it can help to head off the rush to abortions is appealing to a regime that is still on the side of population increase. In Germany, the campaign to legalize abortion is gaining ground, and there is even less hope that it can be diverted by adoption.

It is estimated that 120,000 children are living in institutions in Germany, the majority too old to be easily placed for adoption. As elsewhere, there are queues of adopters, but many obstacles between them and the children.

The German heritage of Roman law has gradually been modified throughout this century, but the conservatism of the agencies is if anything greater than in other countries. Religious matching, prejudice against working mothers, reluctance to allow couples with natural children to adopt, and the suspicion that no family can really accept a child that the agencies think of as hard to place—all these factors add to the difficulty of adoption.

The definition of a 'hard-to-place' child also seems more rigid in Germany than elsewhere. The Danish agency Terre des Hommes reports that the children of foreign workers in Germany are considered to be of mixed race, and therefore unadoptable; Danish families have been adopting them instead. Such children, perhaps half Greek or Turkish, would be easily placed in many other countries; but German prejudice against the *Gastarbeiter*, the foreign workers who are not allowed to bring their families with them to Germany, extends to any children they have while there.

The system of financing the German children's homes also creates obstacles to adoption. The *Länder*, or states, do the adoptive placement; but putting a child in a foster home with a view to adoption costs the state a subsidy during the fostering period. If the child goes to an institution, on the other hand, he is supported by the local authority, and the state pays nothing. The institution in turn receives a stipend based on the number of children in its care, so few efforts are made to reduce the number.

All this produces an almost Italian situation of muddle and conflicting interests, with each party pursuing its own short-term ends and losing sight of the whole picture. However, efforts to place the *Heimkinder* are becoming more insistent in Germany, fuelled by the impatience of would-be adopters. The popular magazine *Brigitte* runs a series with large colour photographs, captioned '*Holt die Kinder aus den Heimen!*' ['Get the children out of the institutions!'] The children featured are either past the adoptable toddler stage or they are slightly physically handicapped—but they are usually very blond.

Children of all races and nationalities are sought after in Scandinavia, where adoption has been so successful that the need for it (as far as the children are concerned) has almost disappeared. The Swedish system of social security, and the famous sexual liberalism that does not stigmatize an unmarried mother, are generally cited as the reasons why scarcely a hundred Swedish children a year are given up for adoption. It may also have something to do with the fact that women's salaries are more nearly equal to those of men than in any other Western country. Every provision is made to help the working mother, from crèches to communal kitchens in apartment blocks.

Scandinavia also shares with England the advantage that when the time came to frame a modern adoption law, there was no tradition of Roman law to dictate its provisions. It could be fully responsive to modern needs. Obligations of mutual support between natural parents and children, and rigid restrictions on the ages of both parties to an adoption, have never been part of the Scandinavian laws. Under most of these laws, any person may apply to take another person as his adopted child. However, the Swedes have shared some of the British reluctance to eradicate the blood tie totally as far as inheritance was concerned.

Adoption as a legal institution has been known in Scandinavia since the late eighteenth century. But the Danish law was not passed until 1923, as part of the work of the inter-Scandinavian commission on family law. Modifications of the law since 1923 include provisions to eliminate the dual relationship of the child to the two sets of parents, and to make an adopted child fully equal to a legitimate one.

Provisions to dissolve an adoption have often been viewed as signs of its incomplete acceptance. But in Scandinavia such provisions are recent additions to the laws and are used to rectify undesirable situations. The parallel with divorce legislation is very striking.

Another provision of the most modern laws is that the child himself is asked for his consent. The age at which this applies descends to 12 in Scandinavia and some American states, and to 10 in the U.S.S.R.

Central Europe—Switzerland, Austria and Luxembourg— has had, in contrast, exceptionally conservative adoption legislation. Only in 1973 was the adopter's age lowered from 40 to 35 in Switzerland; and in Austria to this day, the obligations of the real parents and child to support one another remain unaffected, but for the child the obligation to support its adoptive parents takes precedence.

Luxembourg and Greece take the provision against adopting,

if one has natural children, to its logical conclusion. A family may only adopt one child—for once it has obtained an heir, there is no further need for children.

Traditional morality finds a place in all the European laws. Although a single person may adopt in most countries, two people may not adopt jointly unless they are a married couple. So does the law show its disapproval of unmarried liaisons, not to speak of homosexual couples.

There are two countries where the common practice of religious matching is explicitly prescribed in the law itself. Not surprisingly, they are Israel and Eire. In Eire, an adoptable child must be either illegitimate or orphaned. The severe stigma on illegitimacy, combined with Catholic disapproval of contraceptives (which are still illegal in Eire) has meant that Irish girls often travelled to England to have their babies and place them for adoption. Improvement in the Irish social services, including the passage of an adoption law in 1952, has helped to dry up the baby supply in the U.K.

Israel has a surprisingly conservative adoption law, considering that it was only passed in 1960. This reflects the long absence of adoption in Jewish religious law. The adopters must be over 35 and of the same faith as the child; the new birth certificate issued for an adopted child is practically indistinguishable from the old one, except for the change of name. Adoption is something of a shameful secret; in fact, the law states: 'Unauthorized disclosure of information in relation to an adopter or an adoptee of his parents leading to their identification is punishable with imprisonment for 3 months.' Only in Soviet law is there a similar provision.

The Israeli law of 1960 not only provides for the punishment of a person who reveals particulars about an adoption, but also opens the register of adoptions to adoptees over the age of 18. Thus the concept of secrecy coexists with the idea that the child's origins are ineradicable, and that it is his right to know them.

In Israel the child welfare services are seen as 'an effort to lessen the gap between members of the various social classes and prevent the creation of a new generation of underprivileged children.'[6] The aim is to have not only a complete system of institutions for children without families, but a comprehensive day care and nursery school system open to all children. This,

94

it is hoped, will prevent the break-up of families for economic reasons, and avoid the accusation that adoption favours the well-to-do.

The Israeli state extends the sphere of responsibility almost as widely as do the communist states. Indeed, in the kibbutzim, Israel has created a model of communal child-rearing that appeals deeply to people in many Western countries. At the same time, adoption is explicitly preferred to institutionaliza- tion, and there is a compulsory review of the situation of children in care every two years.

There are by now certain trends to be discerned in the European adoption picture. Everywhere, privileged women are moving from adoption to abortion as a way to avoid raising unwanted children. This is one reason for the dramatic fall in the birth rates of almost all the countries of western Europe. It is rare for a woman to consent to the adoption of her illegiti- mate child, even if she will have difficulty in raising it; on the other hand, abortion is becoming commonplace. The women who choose abortion are not letting religion, law, or moral sanctions stand in their way—they are massively declaring that this is their preferred solution to the problem. Even in Italy, where the new divorce law was almost repealed, figures are quoted of over a million illegal abortions a year.

Children offered for adoption, then, are increasingly those of women who for reasons of fear, poverty, limited access, or tradition cannot manage to obtain abortions; and of women who find after several years that raising children on their own, whether on social security or on the limited salaries women can usually obtain, is insuperably difficult. Children from these sources, are not as easily adoptable as children from the middle-class women who had them and relinquished them in the days before abortion. Race and class, and often age, are obstacles to their placement in the eyes of the agencies, if not in the eyes of the adopters. Campaigns are mounted to find adopters affluent enough to support extra children, but tolerant enough to accept members of a family unlike themselves in colour, health or background.

The idea of these children becoming part of such families is greeted with deep suspicion by the social agencies responsible for the children. Hence the paradoxical situation that the state does not always make efforts to promote adoption, even though it would cost far less than keeping the children in institutions or in foster care.

The countries that are moving towards modern adoption legislation are gradually lowering the required age for adopters; making adoption more complete; and enabling families who already have their own children to adopt others. Countries that have long had such legislation are now engaged in removing some of the secrecy that surrounded adoption, and coming to grips with the bothersome aspects of the legal fiction that adoption has been. They are experimenting with new forms of guardianship; with revocable adoptions; with other ways of legitimating a child born out of wedlock.

The new Adoption Bill being debated in England shows very clearly the conflicting trends in adoption thinking. The Report of the Departmental Committee (known as the Houghton Report) on which it is based, is intended to be a complete overhaul of British adoption legislation, with the aim of making it entirely consistent, flexible, and comprehensive. The report was a compromise, unanimously accepted, among a group of professional adoption workers who were very much aware of the deep social issues they were tackling. It is, at the moment, the most thorough compendium of modern adoption thinking to be found anywhere.

To Dr David Owen, who first attempted to put the provisions of the Houghton Report on the statute book as a Private Member's Bill, its most important article is the requirement that all local authorities do adoption work. This will ensure that children do not remain in care because there is no one responsible for arranging their adoption; it will help to avoid the religious and class bias that many would-be adopters find at present in the private agencies; and it will enable third-party placements, that by-pass the agency network altogether, to be effectively banned. It will also ensure that adoption work is part of a comprehensive social service, and thus can be viewed as part of a whole range of possibilities for the child. The mother will not be pressured into giving her consent to adoption, nor will artificial distinctions be maintained between adoptive and foster placement.

More controversial is the provision that after five years foster parents may apply to adopt without the risk that the natural parents will be able to remove the child before the court hearing. Nor will they be able to do so if they have ever consented to the child's adoption. Many have predicted that this strengthening of the rights of foster parents will lead to parental refusal to allow their children to be fostered, even where it would be in the child's best interests. But the lawmakers have been convinced by the current child welfare orthodoxy—which is accumulating massive evidence in its favour—that psychological continuity is of overriding importance to the young child, and that the person who has become the child's psychological parent should have an indisputable right to continue to care for it.

The Bill has received support from both political parties; although an election intervened to prevent its second reading, it has now (1975) been re-introduced in more complete form by the Government. Measures like adoption legislation tend to go to the wall in the face of more immediate political pressures — a frequent obstacle to their passage. But although time and political upheaval may be continuing roadblocks, the Bill has had few detractors.

One of the few criticisms has been that it is a charter against poor people; that the ban on independent placements and the increasing rights of foster parents will give the middle classes even more weapons against the poor families who cannot prevent their children going into care. To swing the balance away from the natural mother, according to this line of thinking, is to swing it in the direction of greater social inequality. To Dr Owen and the Labour Government of which he is a member, this is a matter of deep concern.

The people who think the natural parents have no rights are just as dangerous as the ones who think the natural parent has every right. If we had a legal cut-off point of six months or a year, what about something like puerperal depression, for example? It may take a year to find the right combination of drugs to clear it up, and if a woman at the end of that time finds that she has lost her baby to a foster-parent, I don't think anyone would suggest that that is fair.[7]

The Houghton Report also contains the suggestion that in the case of adoption by relatives, first consideration should be given to the possibility of legal guardianship. Not only could the confusion of family relationships in a relative adoption be damaging, but adoption by a step-parent is often used in a punitive way, to cut out the rights of the divorced parent.

Goldstein, Freud, and Solnit, in *Beyond the Best Interests of the Child*,[8] suggest that in divorce and custody cases, the parent who is awarded custody of the child should be able to refuse access to the other parent, in the name of consistency and continuity. This kind of thing, like step-parent adoption, is open to abuse as a weapon in the battles between adults, who will not always use it with the child's interests in mind.

Another way in which the climate around adoption is changing is in the matter of access to the child's original identity. Adopted children themselves are often anxious to have more information about their first parents than is provided by their adopters, and sometimes even wish to trace and meet them. The Houghton Report agrees that the secrecy surrounding adoption has diminished in recent years, and recommends that adoptees over 18 should be allowed access to their original birth certificates. Further information can be made available at the court's discretion.

There are other changes taking place in British adoption thinking that are not reflected in the law. The pendulum is swinging away from giving preference to childless couples, to such an extent that they may soon feel that they are being discriminated against. English law has never banned adoption by people who already have children, but many agencies have done so in the past. The present emphasis on placing the hard-to-place children has led many agencies to recruit people with their own children, in the belief that they will be more tolerant and less narcissistic in their demands than will the childless. The long-held assumption that people unable to have their own children would feel an extra desire for them, and thus make the best adopters, is being suddenly jettisoned, as is the notion that it is unfair to expect an adopted child to compete with a natural one. Raissa Page, deputy director of the A.B.A.A., has said:

We now feel that no couple has a right to a child but every child has the right to have parents, and the best possible parents at that. What we are saying is unpopular and some people who are quite worthy may have to go by default. But our first duty must be to the child. We cannot accept responsibility for meeting the problems of infertility.[9]

Another movement in opinion, rather than law, is that in favour of terminating the rights of parents whose children have been in the care of the authorities for more than a year or two, and who show little sign of being able to rehabilitate their families. This movement received its main impetus from Jane Rowe's 1973 report, *Children Who Wait*. This major A.B.A.A. project set out to answer the question, 'Are there children in care who need permanent substitute parents?' Children numbering 2,812, in the care of both local authorities and voluntary agencies, were studied. The fact emerged that if a child of primary school age or below had been in care for six months, he had only one chance in four of returning to his family before he reached school-leaving age. Three-quarters of the children in the study had been in care for two or more years.

The authors of the report estimated that there were probably at least 6,000 children in care in the country as a whole who needed substitute families. However, they warn eager adopters, 'among the 626 children (in the study) found waiting for families, there was only one healthy white baby in need of parents and one other baby whose only problem seemed to be his racial background.'[10] Two-thirds of the children were of school age, one in four was coloured, and more than half were living with siblings who should be placed with them. 'Behaviour problems were noted more frequently than any other difficulty, but below average intelligence appeared to be a more serious obstacle to placement.'[11] Many of the natural parents were opposed to the child's placement, but many children who had come into care as babies had no contact at all with parents. And any contact at all seemed to be better than none, no matter what the qualities of the parents.

Two fairly distinct categories of children emerged from the study: (a) single illegitimate children, and (b) sibling

99

groups from disorganised families. The illegitimate children tended to come into care as babies, have little contact with parents and stay a very long time unless adopted. Many of them were boarded out. The family groups came in and out of care more often, had more contact with parents and were less likely to remain in care throughout their childhood. The parents of many of these legitimate children had serious personality difficulties which limited their capacity to act as parents, but on the whole the children themselves had fewer problems than the illegitimate children in the study.[12]

The adoptive placement of the 'children who wait' is a complicated matter. That they are in care by no means indicates that they are free for adoption. In fact the separation of children from their families is related to other social problems — the housing shortage for example, as Bowlby makes clear:

> A situation has arisen in the United Kingdom in which it is legally possible for parents who have been evicted for not paying their rent to leave the children in the care of a local authority and to find accommodation for themselves where children are not accepted. In one area this accounts for about 33 per cent of the children in care.[13]

It is probably possible to generalize from Jane Rowe's findings, and to use them to explain the situation in many European countries. The children in care are separated from would-be adopters by many obstacles not just legal and traditional: they are not easily placeable like the illegitimate babies born to young girls that the agencies are used to handling.

To overcome these obstacles requires not only education of the adopting public and commitment on the part of social workers. It also demands that the questions raised in *Beyond the Best Interests of the Child* be clearly faced. Is society willing to further penalize deprived parents in order to avoid the risk of depriving their children? Many would now say that early permanent placement of children from such families is necessary to cut through the so-called cycle of deprivation. But the people responsible for such action, whether social workers or judges, are deterred by the political implications of the problem.

We shall see how the class questions raised by adoption become largely racial questions in the United States, where adoption is more generally accepted and more widely practised than in any other country. In 1970, the last year for which statistics are available, 175,000 children were adopted. As in Europe, however, adoption faces new obstacles and raises new questions.

It has been pointed out that supply and demand are difficult to estimate, because they have been controlled by social workers' perceptions. The child accepted for surrender is one estimate of supply; the family accepted for adoptive placement is one estimate of demand. Both figures exclude many who would be included if the question were differently defined. In some agencies, only 30 per cent of mothers who make inquiries are finally allowed to relinquish their babies; and potential adopters may be deterred even before they inquire, by rumours about the baby shortage.

Census-based estimates of 350,000 children in the care of service agencies, and 2,378,000 children living apart from their parents, have convinced the advocates of adoption that the services now being provided to children are totally inadequate, and that the official figures of adoptable children show only the tip of an iceberg. Far from trying to wrench children away from families that want to keep them, adopters see themselves as playing a much-needed role in the lives of children who have long ceased to have any contact with their original families.

Adoptive parents are quite aware of the reasons why children come into care, as 4th N.A.C.A.C. recognized:

Most neglected children in publicly financed substitute care are children of the poor, often the poor on welfare. They are usually young and usually from single-parent families in which an ill-educated woman is trying to raise a large family by herself. Many of these parents not only agree to placements but seek them and seek them repeatedly as a means of coping with the crises of a marginal existence.[14]

Aid to Families with Dependent Children (A.F.D.C.) has been the main government response to preventing family break-up under such circumstances; but, 'If only cash income is counted, 43 per cent of this group remain in poverty.'[15]

The 4th Conference was heavily influenced by *Beyond the Best Interests of the Child*. This work has popularized the idea that child placement should be handled as an emergency, because the child's sense of time cannot cope with long delays; it also argues that, in most custody cases, there is no perfect solution or best interest—instead, the 'least detrimental alternative' should be sought. But the adopters who attended the conference were very careful not to use these ideas as a sort of adopter's charter —they recommended that court termination of parental rights should not be granted until

> after the agency has demonstrated a serious attempt to reconstitute the family through application of services ... Termination must not be a punishment for being poor. In the instance of low income families who other than for financial reasons would be able to retain their children, the possibility that their children could wind up adopted with a subsidy is particularly repugnant.[16]

Adoptive parents in the United States are increasingly aware of themselves as an 'ethnic minority', and they use the terms that other such groups have made current: 'participation', 'consciousness raising', and so on.

Just as adoptive families are surprisingly similar to the defenders of legalized abortion, American adopters are champions of the rights of many groups who might seem, at first glance, to be their natural enemies. Far from attacking the women's movement, with its insistence that the unmarried mother be helped to keep her child, adoptive parents are urging that adoption agencies provide complete casework services, including help for single parents. Equally, they are asking that single people be allowed to adopt. Adoptive families themselves tend to be egalitarian, and the agencies' frequent requirement that adopting mothers quit their jobs is also being challenged.

One of the most revolutionary movements in American adoption is that of committing far greater resources to rapid placement and active casework, so that no child can be lost in the system. It seems expensive to establish such a scheme, but the experience of the Los Angeles County Department of Adoptions has been influential in convincing others that it can be done:

> Los Angeles County, through a program of identifying and placing children in permanent homes, has figured a savings of *10 million* dollars during the period 1970–72 from what continued care would have cost. $100,000 [the price of a computerised 'tracking system'] to save *10 million* dollars is a logic that can be sold to any legislature.[17]

This may be a resurgence of the cost-benefit thinking behind the administration of the Poor Laws, but if so it has changed out of all recognition.

5 Eastern Contrasts

The most obvious means by which European ideas about adoption have been disseminated is colonialism. We have seen how the United States, Australia, and Canada were the direct inheritors of English traditions of social welfare (with a French influence in some areas), and how the imported ideas were modified to suit different conditions.

In these colonies, it was an abundance of land and a scarcity of population that led to greater acceptance of adoption. There was no conflict between imported and native values, because contact between the settlers and the indigenous population was minimal and hostile. This was not true of the English colonies in Asia and Africa, where the new lawmakers could not entirely modify the traditional way of life of the peoples they were governing.

The compromises produced by this situation are still reflected in law. Sarawak, for example, requires (as does English law) that the adopter be at least 21, and 20 years older than the child he adopts, but:

> Before registering the adoption by a person of the Muslim faith the District Officer must draw his attention clearly and unmistakably to the fact that adoption is contrary to the Hukum Shara ...
>
> The Governor in Council may make rules to regulate adoption of heirs by heads of Chinese families according to Chinese custom, and to regulate adoption of adults among races in which such adoptions are recognised by custom.[1]

The law of Botswana and Lesotho concludes that 'Adoption of

an African child by Africans under native law and custom is not affected or prevented by this proclamation.'[2]

Cultural clashes can also be traced in the adoption laws. The conflict in Canada between French Catholics and English Protestants means that Quebec, alone among the Canadian provinces, requires that adoptive parents must 'profess the religious faith to which the child belongs by baptism'.

Imperialism then has been one major way of bringing the laws and customs of very disparate areas into line with the ideas of the dominant Western countries.

But it has not been the only modernizing influence on traditional patterns. Communist revolution, in Eastern Europe and in Asia, has been perhaps the most dramatic means of social change the world has seen in this century. Its effect on law and on social organization has been, in intention at least, very nearly total.

The Soviet Union is now losing some of its primacy as the world's leading example of socialist practice, but for the first half of this century, other countries looked to the U.S.S.R. to see how these ideas would work themselves out. As far as adoption was concerned, the message was ambiguous.

Traditional Slavic society had much in common with the feudalism of Western Europe, which was, as we have seen, inhospitable to adoption.

Among the Slavs there has never been a solidary and corporate kin group but, rather, that loose assemblage known to ethnographers as the bilateral kindred ... the traditional concentration of loyalty as much upon the household work group as upon the family proper prepared the people for the new arrangements which were inaugurated under the Soviet system.[3]

Feudalism and 'loyalty to the work group' do not always imply hostility to adoption; in Japan, the recognition of strong social ties other than familial ones seems to have helped adoption to be widely accepted.

The application of socialist principles also dictates that there are stronger claims than those of blood. If hereditary rule is replaced by the rule of those who do the work, and the bourgeois family replaced by the collective, should not a child belong to the person who cares for it? Brecht's *Caucasian Chalk Circle*, for example, is about the fostering of a royal baby by a peasant woman who rescues it when its royal parents flee the Revolution and forget to take the baby with them. When it becomes the key to an inheritance, the natural parents try to reclaim the child — but a peasant judge has come to power. In a version of the Judgment of Solomon, the woman who has loved and raised the child refuses to try to pull him out of the chalk circle. The judge concludes,

> What there is shall go to those who are
>   good for it,
> Children to the motherly, that they prosper,
> Carts to good drivers, that they be driven well,
> The valley to the waterers, that it yield fruit.[4]

Marx and Engels, however, believed that the family was counter-revolutionary, produced by capitalism and reinforcing it. Weakening of the blood tie might in theory pave the way for adoption, but not if adoption itself simply tried to reproduce the family it had replaced. The Soviet state attempted to substitute itself for the family in many areas, although there is some debate about whether the early Bolsheviks actually intended to abolish it. Their enemies claimed that 'the Bolsheviks believe in the nationalization of women' — the idea that they believed in the destruction of any tie between parents and children is probably just as untrue.

However, early socialist thought was certainly unfavourable to adoption. The first Soviet legal code, in 1918, actually abolished it, and it was not legalized again until 1926. Not only was it thought that the state would take over most of the functions of the family, at least as far as homeless children were concerned, but the whole notion of transmission of status through the family was under attack. This, of course, applied to inheritance of wealth as much as to inheritance of those attitudes transmitted through a family upbringing. Inheritance, too, was abolished in 1918 for estates of over 10,000 roubles.

The early notions of the Bolsheviks were modified in many areas in subsequent years. The level of permitted inheritance was gradually raised, so that today there is only a tax comparable to that in Western countries. Adoption, too, has reasserted itself, although there are other reasons for its comparative lack of popularity.

A major reason for the necessity of reintroducing adoption was simply that the state was not equipped to replace the family. There were not enough institutions to house even genuine orphans, let alone children with any semblance of a family. There were perhaps several million homeless children after the civil war; the savage bands of orphans who roamed the countryside convinced the authorities of the necessity of temporarily at least strengthening the family. The desire to keep the birth-rate up, to replace Russia's decimated population, did the rest.

Vast movements of people, such as the dispossessed kulaks, added to the disintegration of families and the need for substitute care: 'Kulak children were often adopted, taken in by more fortunate relatives or neighbors, or added to the population of homeless children.'[5]

The Soviet family itself, however, was under such strain from a variety of sources that adoption, even when possible, was not always attractive. Soviet women did two jobs: the care of the household (still not shared by men) and outside employment, which was both an ideological and a practical necessity. Many families lived in one-room quarters, and most shared cooking facilities. Such arrangements made one child, or no children, the preferred family size. The Government has tried to keep the birth-rate up by means ranging from the discouragement of divorce to the awarding of medals to heroine mothers with large families—the size of the effort put into such encouragement indicates the strength of the opposing forces.

Strain on the family has been alleviated by communal arrangements like factory and neighbourhood canteens, by extended-day and boarding schools for children, by moving much of social life outside the home. Families with children have also continued to make use of a persistent Russian institution: the granny system. Like the care of children, the care of the aged has been slow in coming from the state. There are simply not enough facilities to take over this function from the family, where it has always rested. One source of opposition to adoption has been that Russian children are obliged by law to support their parents, and this provision has been carried over into the Soviet constitution. Nor is it simply a law that exists on paper — it is very much a part of everyday life.

> Perhaps Engels would not have approved, but the fact is that in the transition period the old folks took over in the Soviet family the functions that he felt were properly those of the socialist state, and the Soviet family often took over a function that he somehow completely overlooked, the care of the aged.[6]

The survival of the Russian family looks like outlasting the transition period. There is growing evidence that in the Soviet Union, as elsewhere, the institutional care of children produces anti-social results. Moreover, it is not the preference of the majority of parents: the new 'extended-day' schools are much more popular than boarding schools. The desire of parents to rear their own children is now receiving official sanction. *Pravda* said in 1969:

> Children are not only the hope and future support of their parents but also the future of our state. Therefore, the raising and care of children should be regarded not as merely the private concern of married couples but as socially useful labour ... [7]

It is evident from this that the family has even been given some new roles—not only are the parents supposed to do most of the usual child-rearing tasks, but they are expected to raise good socialist citizens in the full sense of the word; to inculcate patriotism and co-operativeness.

The family has much help in performing these complex tasks. Communal responsibility for children has always been a feature of Russian life, and its institutionalization has thus built on a feeling that was already powerful. Urie Bronfenbrenner, in his comparison of Soviet and American child-rearing methods, describes the effects of this:

> Given this diffusion of nurturant behaviour toward children, it is hardly surprising that Soviet youngsters

exhibit less anxiety than their American age-mates when their mother leaves them in the care of another person or in a nursery.[8]

A new facet is added to the meaning of the word 'adoption' by this sort of collective responsibility.

> through the system of *shevstvo*, perhaps best described as 'group adoption', each class takes on responsibility for the upbringing of a group of children at a lower grade level. For example, a fourth grade class 'adopts' a first grade class in the same school; the older children escort the younger ones to school, play with them in the school yard, teach them new games, read to them, help them with schoolwork —in general, act as older brothers and sisters ... Finally, the system of 'adoption' embraces adult collectives in the outside world so that each school may also be a 'ward' of a shop in a factory, or of a bureau of a municipal agency, with the workers devoting their spare time to activities with or in behalf of 'our class' at the neighborhood school.[9]

This kind of support from the community at large may help to prevent family break-up; but there are still many children who need substitute families, and Soviet law allows them—indeed, encourages them—to be placed for adoption. Parents may lose their rights in a child if it has been in the care of the state for a year, during which they have shown no interest in it. Parental rights may be vested in the child care agency, which then transfers them to the adopting parents. This 'general consent to adoption' has proved its utility in many states of the United States, and is part of the proposed Adoption Bill in England.

One of the functions of adoption in the Soviet Union, as in the West, is legitimation—but this poses problems in periods when divorce is difficult to obtain. A man may have a family by his wife and a new family by a woman he is unable to marry —but if his legal wife will not consent to a divorce, she is unlikely to consent to his adoption and legitimation of the other woman's children.

Adoption also suffers from the misunderstandings that arise from its being a legal creation, rather than a part of Russian tradition accepted and understood by all. Legitimation by adoption, in particular, seems an absurdity—a view that, as we have seen, Western legislators are taking more seriously these days.

> Here is a harassed father at the Odessa administration of the Ukrainian Ministry of Justice. Officials tell him that to give his son his name he must adopt the child. There is no other way. 'But, comrades, look, it's my little son—my son. Here I am before you—his father. How then can I adopt my own son?'[10]

The family seems safe now as a part of Soviet life, and with it the institution of adoption. Convergence seems to be occurring in child care as in so many other areas, and the Soviet move away from boarding nurseries and schools, and the American move to extend state day care of children, are producing parallel situations. The future ideal in both countries seems to be a family for every child, combined with much greater state sharing of the practical aspects of child-rearing.

The Soviet adoption law, although very advanced in many respects, still shows its doubts about adoption in its insistence on secrecy. The birthplace of the child, and even the date of birth, can be changed on the new birth certificate to make tracing of the natural parents more difficult. It is illegal to disclose the fact of an adoption against the wishes of the adopters.

But basically, Soviet law nowadays concerns itself with the same matters that are vexing every industrialized country: the termination of parental rights over children in care, measuring the wishes of adopters and natural parents against the needs of children.

The adoption legislation in Eastern Europe is almost entirely a mirror of Soviet law, although there are some differences that reflect the various countries' legal traditions. In Romania, for example, the only Warsaw Pact country to have inherited the legal traditions of the Roman Empire, the child's rights of inheritance in his natural family have been retained.

The social function of adoption, as of all parenthood, is emphasized in the legislation of all the socialist countries as it is in the U.S.S.R. In Romania a child cannot be adopted 'with a view to exploiting him or for other purposes contrary to the law or to the rules of socialist life'. While in Czechoslovakia, 'only citizens whose standard of living is a guarantee that the adoption will benefit the child and society may become adoptive parents.'

The conscious encouragement of a healthy society is the new element in these laws, and it may be the contribution that this part of the world makes to international adoption thinking: Bronfenbrenner argues that the Soviet eagerness to make good citizens fills what in the United States is a vacuum leading to delinquency. The abdication of Western parents from their socializing role is in sharp contrast to the seriousness with which it is taken in the U.S.S.R.; ironically, the West may abolish the family long before the Soviets do.

We have seen the state's ambivalence about adoption when it attempts to apply socialist principles to a country with no tradition of adoption. China is in a very different situation: what is perhaps the world's longest unbroken tradition of adoption has meshed into the Chinese version of agrarian communism. The *canard* that revolution means the abolition of the family receives its death-blow here.

As recently as the 1940s, sections of Chinese society could be found in every stage of transition between the traditional family based society and the new forms brought about by the impact of capitalist imperialism and socialist revolution. Some aspects of the old system fitted quite well into the new, but others were radically changed.

Concubinage was officially disapproved by the Revolution, but in any case it was only practised in some parts of China. Nowhere did concubines have status equal to that of wives, although the child of a concubine might be preferred as heir to a child from outside the clan. The system of relative adoption as practised in Shantung Province was described in 1948:

Adoption, rather than concubinage, solves the problem of childless wives ... Adoption is closely related to inheritance. As long as the deceased has a son, the problem of adoption does not arise, but if a man has no son, the adoption of an heir is imperative. The male line must be continued. The adopted heir is always the next of kin, or the father's brother's son ... When a brother's son is not available, the choice falls on the next nearest kin in the patrilineal line. Adopting a member from the matrilineal line, such as a wife's brother's son, is unknown, but custom allows a son-in-law to take a real son's place in continuing the family line. In such a case, the daughter of the family will marry her husband at her parents' home. The husband and their children will take her family's name.[11]

Here is another analogy between marriage and adoption: marrying into the family is sometimes exactly equivalent to being adopted into it.

In other parts of China, the practice of modern adoption — that is, the adoption of strangers — provided an alternative to concubinage. Olga Lang (1946) tells the story of a modern wife whose husband was urged by his mother to take a concubine, since his marriage was childless; rather than have this happen, the wife feigned pregnancy and went to another city to adopt a baby. In other cases, it is the wife herself who urges her husband to take a concubine; once he has a child, her own position is not so severely threatened.

But other forms of adoption existed in China before the revolution, although probably none were so widely practised as the adoption of a related heir. Lang reports that in the village she studied, the consent of the clan head (who officiated at ancestor worship) was necessary for the adoption of an heir: 'The difference between the status of boys adopted as legal heirs and adopted "out of charity" was abolished by the legal code but was still observed generally: the legal heir had to be a member of one's clan.'[12]

Obviously some charitable adoption was practised even in traditional China. The adoption of a daughter-in-law in her childhood has also been made illegal, but the desire to have many children in one's household meant that adoption was often practised even when one already had a son: 'Maids sometimes became concubines, and young servants were even adopted into the family on account of exceptional talent or merit.'[13] This way, families with property acquired more children, while the landless tended to lose some of theirs.

Today, government propaganda urges people to postpone marriage until 25 or 30 and to practise contraception thereafter. The official attitude is that this is to free people for productive labour, rather than because of specific worry about population size — but it is certainly true that the state would have taken over many more of the family's functions if there had not been simply too many children for this to be practicable.

Although, as in the U.S.S.R., state day care is the recommended solution for working mothers, the granny system is still almost universal. However, other communal arrangements — for cooking and laundry, for example — make the combination of family life with outside work easier than it is probably anywhere else in the world.

Population growth is still a problem in China, in spite of official disclaimers — and the Asian desire for many children, seen in the popularity of adoption, is being consciously discouraged. When the journalist K. S. Karol interviewed the Director of the Department of Women in Peking, she told him that:

> the survival of the old concept of the family is the main obstacle to general acceptance of birth control. Until not so long ago, in the rural areas having children was considered something of an investment, an insurance against old age. Today the state looks after old people, but such deeply ingrained attitudes are not so quickly overcome.[14]

This desire for parenthood, however, has another side; it can be turned to good use, particularly when it is combined with a long tradition of adoption. The Director continued,

> If you know how much we love children in our country, you will fully understand that there is no father who would not marry the mother of his child. We have no problems of that kind, just as we have no abandoned children or even orphans. Yes, children who have lost their parents are always adopted by a family close to them which is given official help.[15]

This interestingly corresponds with another kind of adoption which is only now gaining ground in the West: subsidized adoption. The communal sense of responsibility for children that is one of the strongest characteristics of Chinese society is only imperfectly realized elsewhere.

While the adoption of non-relatives—which was practised to a limited degree in pre-revolutionary China—is now gaining ground, this does not mean that the ties of blood are being correspondingly weakened: although most university students and sons of urban families are sent to work in the countryside, since the Government's aim is to redistribute the population and counteract urbanization, exemption can be sought for only sons. In a recent celebrated case, an only son refused such exemption after being re-educated in the 'criticize Confucius' campaign, and urged his parents to accept his viewpoint.

The West's main interest in Asian adoption comes about because of the demand for babies from other countries, now that the home-produced supply has dwindled so drastically. China is out of the running as far as international adoption is concerned—and according to the Chinese, this is not only because the 'bamboo curtain' would prevent such movement, but because there are no children in China without families or substitute families.

If this is indeed true, it is a complete contrast to the situation in India, Pakistan, and most of South-East Asia, and notoriously in South Korea and South Vietnam. Even Japan has an unwanted child problem, although in-country adoption is the most likely solution to it. Only in China has the earlier situation of massive numbers of orphans and homeless children been totally reversed.

Japan presents us with the third example for our Asian typology. The U.S.S.R. shows us Westernization and socialism grafted on to a society with no previous tradition of adoption; China shows us what happens when a tradition of adoption becomes incorporated into socialism. Japan also had a Buddhist tradition of adoption, similar to that in China; but it met the impact of Western-style capitalism in the years before adoption was accepted in the West. The result has been a confusing and ambiguous blend of practices and attitudes, some operating for adoption and some against it.

114

Archaic Japan is often said to have had a feudal system—but instead of taking the place of family relationships, including adoptive ones, as in Western Europe, Japanese feudalism seems to have intensified and even created family ties. As late as the sixteenth and seventeenth centuries in England, the prosperous rural household included many unrelated people. In Japan, the relationships created by this means often became adoptive ones. *Yoshi* is the Japanese term for adoption of a tenant or retainer—a practice that had a long-standing tradition behind it. In one community, Ishigami in northern Japan, 'Families which entered the community later were able to settle there only by entering into adoptive relationships with the wealthy Saito family.'[16] In other words, an immigrant family had to give the local feudal lords children to increase their work-force, in return for feudal patronage.

Adoption of an adult who had proven himself an appropriate heir, a practice we have noted in ancient Rome, also occurred in Japan: 'adoption was one important mode of ascent in Japan. A father might even disinherit a son in order to adopt a talented young man. However, the individual so chosen rose alone.'[17]

In Japan as in England, feudalism and primogeniture helped to create the necessary conditions for rapid industrialization. The amassing of capital was facilitated by the social system, and those without land provided a mobile work-force.

Under European feudalism, work-mates and age-mates to some extent supplanted the family. In Japan to this day, age groups seem to take the place of family groups. Businessmen, schoolchildren, housewives spend much time in groups of their own kind. Factories and companies are notoriously paternalistic on every level: '*oyabun-kobun*: a leader, such as a work-gang foreman, becomes a symbolic parent, "adopting" his adult followers ritually.'[18]

As in China, heir adoption in Japan was preferably done within the kin group. The rapid changes wrought by industrialization produced in Japan, as elsewhere, broken families and unwanted children—but the children abandoned by one family were not necessarily adoptable by another. The stigma of illegitimacy was (and still is) very strong, and any family who adopted an unknown child did their best to conceal his origins.

The family register of an unmarried woman records the fact

that she has had a child and given it up for adoption, thus jeopardizing her chances of marriage. Abortion is practised in Japan almost up to the end of pregnancy—few girls want to risk the ostracism of bearing the child, and the Government has encouraged abortion as a means of population control. The adoptive parents, too, consider adoption to be a shameful secret: there are up to 3,000 court cases every year involving foster parents who have falsely registered adopted children as born to them.

When the deception is revealed, the fictive family tie is not preserved. In one recent case, two women learned that their 20-year-old sons had been inadvertently exchanged in the hospital nursery at birth. The grown-up boys were reunited with their original families, since: 'According to judicial precedents, once a child–parent relationship proves to be false, it should be dissolved despite the fact that the child and its parents have been living as real child and parents for many years.'[19]

Changes in the adoption laws have been proposed to allow childless couples to register adopted children as their own and to expunge the name of the natural mother from the adoption records. Doctors believe that this will help to avert dangerously late abortions by making the mothers willing to carry their babies to term and place them for adoption.

The professor of law who is campaigning for the changes says that:

> foster parents are haunted by the fear that their children might know the facts of their birth during their formative years and be dealt a devastating psychological blow.
>
> In fact there are many cases in which such children have taken to juvenile delinquency or killed themselves in extreme cases after they came to know that they were adopted children ... [20]

There can be no clearer statement than this of the lack of popular acceptance of non-relative adoptions in Japan.

There are other opponents to easier adoption in Japan, and some indications that if women who now seek abortions choose to have their babies, adopters may be in short supply. The

116

Japanese industrial juggernaut claims to be short of almost a million workers, and is trying to influence the Government to tighten restrictions on abortion (the pill is still illegal). But they are running into opposition from housewives and women's liberation groups, who point out that 30 per cent of the families in Japan live in one-room flats, and that suicide is frequent among young housewives who cannot stand their bird-cage existence. The stresses of urbanization and industrial concentration are blamed for another alarming trend, the abandonment of children (some 150 cases a year) and infanticide (around 200).

The desire for children in every Asian country has to contend with fears about population growth. It may be that the population explosion in poor countries has been in part the result of Western attitudes grafted on to traditional societies, without the concomitant Western resources and social structure. For example, the elimination of infanticide, especially of girl babies, ended one method of population control in India and China. And it is well known that efforts to increase life expectancy by reducing infant mortality and controlling epidemics were succeeding long before birth control was officially sanctioned. Gunnar Myrdal's vast study of population and poverty in South Asia notes that: 'In India, the population seems to have been virtually stationary in the two thousand years preceding the colonial era.'[21]

If adoption is viewed as the opponent of abortion, there is little doubt, in Asia at least, which institution will have to give way. At present, the only countries that are controlling their populations are doing so by means of abortion. According to an I.U.C.W. report:

After the war, in 1948, Japan passed a law permitting abortions for economic reasons as well as for reasons of the mother's health. Under this 'Eugenic Protection Law' abortions rose to a peak of more than 1,170,000 officially reported in 1955, then gradually diminished to a reported total of some 740,000 in 1971 ...

In China, a general policy of family planning is encouraged and the minimum age for marriage is 18 for women and 20 for men. Abortions by suction are made ...

117

the aim is to arrive at a demographic increase of 1% per annum by the year 2000.[22]

Compare this with India, where a liberalized abortion law was not introduced until April 1973, and where the population is growing at 3 per cent a year.

> After 20 years of planned growth, India is effectively moving backwards ... the number falling below the (poverty) line (£2 a month) may already have exceeded half the population of 570 million.[23]

Abortion is not the only factor in population control. A United Nations expert at the Bucharest Population Conference of August 1974 identified the two social components of 'explosive' population growth: a society in which women have no role other than reproduction, and in which wealth is very unequally distributed.

These conditions are found in many of the South American countries that are beginning to export children to the international adoption market. Dom Moraes, in his report for the U.N. on world population, found that the birth-rate in Colombia is twice that desired by the women themselves. The population is controlled, if at all, by illegal abortion. The Director of the U.N. Information Centre in Bogota explained it this way:

> If you take the pill, or you have the I.U.D., this is a process which continues. You can't go to the priest and confess unless you stop the methods. Abortion is a single act. You can go and confess to an abortion and the priest will give you prayers to say and forgive you. I think this is why there are so many abortions in Latin America.[24]

This report saw *machismo*, male dominance, as another obstacle to population control. This hypothesis has been advanced about other oppressed groups with a high birth-rate—the black population of the United States, for example. The argument is that when a man has been stripped of all sources of pride except his virility, he will use that to prove himself powerful and capable.

But to point to *machismo* as a reason for an exploding population only pushes it back a step—it can be traced further, to the economic causes of this mentality. The Western countries have found that prosperity lowers the birth-rate: people who do not need children for old-age insurance, or to prove themselves, begin thinking of a family as an economic drain. They turn to abortion and birth control, whether or not these options are legally and morally sanctioned. An exception to this trend is those rich families that think of themselves as dynasties; ironically, Rose Kennedy was using the logic of the Indian peasant when she said, 'If I had not had nine children, I would not have a son today.'

On the whole, however, state insurance obviates the need for personal insurance in the form of a large family; and this is the process that will have to occur in the poor countries before their population is finally controlled, unless they take the socialist alternative. Even if the strictest controls went into effect immediately, however, it would still be many years before zero population growth is achieved; and by that time, adopters may have begun defining their roles quite differently. The Western baby famine need not affect the argument for birth control in the developing world.

6 Inter-country Adoption

Send these, the homeless, tempest-tossed to me;
I lift my lamp beside the golden door.

poem on the Statue of Liberty,
New York Harbour.

The great number of orphans left after the First World War induced many of the Western countries to pass or revive adoption laws. After the Second World War, the movement to rescue the children of the devastated countries was even stronger. Every country was concerned to rehabilitate its own, rather than to lose yet another generation; it was only in the countries occupied by foreign armies for long after the war that inter-country adoption became one solution to the problem.

The U.S.S.R., Britain, and France all set up programmes to find homes for their orphaned or displaced children; international agencies worked to reunite families. Jewish children fostered by non-Jewish families were returned to their surviving relatives.

The occupied nations of Germany, Japan, Italy, and Greece became the main sources of children for international adoption. In part, this was because soldiers of the occupying armies were aware of the problem and sometimes in contact with the children, and through them foreign governments became aware of it too. There was no mechanism to facilitate inter-country adoption in the absence of such a foreign garrison.

Retribution towards the countries that had lost the war also played its part in preventing the large-scale effort necessary to rehabilitate families. Institutions were set up for the children, but little real concern was shown for their welfare. A social worker for International Social Service said:

> In occupied Germany any soldier who was relatively sober could go into an orphanage and say 'I'll have that one.' Boys were sometimes adopted for homosexual purposes, and they would take 12-year-old girls and use them as maids.[1]

Rich families looking for a child to adopt went to the countries that would not say no to a representative of the rich and generous United States. Southern Italy and Greece were well-known hunting-grounds.

For all this, the number of children adopted by foreign nationals was not very large—perhaps slightly more than 500 entered the United States in any one year. These were the years when the illegitimacy rate was rising at home, and in most areas there was no shortage of adoptable babies.

It was the Korean War that brought inter-country adoption fully into the American national consciousness. The half-Asian children of the American soldiers became the responsibility of the occupying army, since many of their mothers were unwilling and—above all—unable to raise them.

Why did this not happen on the same scale in Japan after the Second World War? Why was it Korea that precipitated this state of affairs, which has since been repeated on a smaller scale in other countries?

To find the answers to these questions, it is first necessary to trace the process of increasing American hegemony in the West, and the increasing underdevelopment of its client states.

Military involvement or a large foreign community seem to be the necessary catalysts to bring about inter-country adoption, since they provide access to adopters. But the adopters thus discovered must have access to adoptable children, and this means that there must be a pool of children whose own families —and whose own country—are unable to keep them.

Bowlby and other authorities see the dislocation produced by industrial society, which breaks up extended families and moves the population into overcrowded cities, as the major cause of large numbers of children needing substitute care. But the Western countries he considers also have, at least in part, the means to deal with the problem: social security, adoption and fostering programmes, temporary institutions.

When such dislocation happens in a nation or community without such resources, an identifiable problem exists that attracts the attention of international relief agencies, including adoption agencies. Some countries, especially in the aftermath of war, are temporarily unable to take care of their own displaced children; but the momentum of economic development eventually means that they can be absorbed. As the country's prosperity increases, its birth-rate declines and population growth becomes more manageable. People are more interested in adopting as they become better-off, and there are at the same time fewer unwanted children born. Those who are available for fostering or adoption experience fewer delays in placement.

An underdeveloped country, on the other hand, experiences an exploding population simultaneously with a decrease in economic capacity—a vicious circle from which it is terribly difficult to escape. There have been many theorists of this syndrome, and it is now generally accepted in the Third World itself that a client relationship to the capitalist metropolis causes such underdevelopment—and the more 'development' aid is poured into a client country, the less self-sufficient it becomes. This thesis is spelt out by André Gunder Frank, who studied its workings in Latin America.

What can be said with confidence, because the historical evidence is clear, is that neither Chile nor any other country in the world which had already previously been firmly incorporated into the world capitalist system as a satellite has, since the nineteenth century, managed to escape from this status to achieve economic development by relying only on national capitalism. The new countries which have developed since then had, like the United States, Canada and Australia, already achieved substantial internal and external economic independence, or like Germany and most significantly Japan had never been satellites, or like the Soviet Union have broken out of the world capitalist system by socialist revolution. Notably, these now more or less developed countries were not richer when they began their development than was Chile when it made its attempt to do the same. But—and this I believe is the crucial distinction—they were not already underdeveloped.[2]

To Frank, underdevelopment is what happens when a national economy is skewed in the direction of producing a surplus of wealth for its exploiters (whether they are inside or outside of the country) rather than producing the necessities of life for its own population and having a share in the lucrative manufacturing that supports the affluence of the developed countries. So the more thoroughly integrated a country is into the world capitalist system, and the more its exports and primary products are needed by the United States and the countries of Western Europe, the worse off its people will be. Aid, tied to the purchase of the manufactures of the donor countries, will exacerbate this underdevelopment; so will injections of foreign capital.

For 'escaping from satellite status to achieve economic development' in Frank's text, one could substitute escaping from dependency, family break-up, and personal poverty and homelessness to achieve a unified social system able to care for its own members. For it is only the developed countries that have in this century been able to care for their own children—and then only for the children of the groups that form part of the capitalist world, not for the children of the satellite groups within the developed countries. Even in the most affluent parts of the world, there are patches of underdevelopment and consequent inability to care for children—one thinks of American blacks, southern Italians, the *Gastarbeiter* of Germany.

This is why the inter-country adoption that followed the world wars was temporary—the crises of dislocation that it sought to alleviate were merely temporary checks in the development of the child-exporting countries. International adoption from South Korea has now been going on for more than twenty years, because war relief has merged into the relief of underdevelopment itself, a pattern which is likely to be the major rationale for inter-country adoption from now on.

South Vietnam attempted to reject much of the help of inter-country adopters because it did not want to become another

Korea. What happened in Korea to deter other countries from travelling the same route? To the adopters of Korean children in other countries, all that has happened is that a few lives have been saved that might otherwise have been lost, and a few children made happy who would otherwise have grown up loveless and delinquent.

Indeed, a 1971 study reports that:

> There is no evidence that the success of placing children from overseas into American homes, or European, is substantially different from that of placing American or European children born in their own country.[3]

Adoption works, but it only works for a few children. The same report estimates that the total number of South Korean children placed overseas was at the time about 11,000. This was a small percentage of the homeless children, who were mostly in institutions. From about 3,000 in institutions in 1945, the number climbed to a peak of almost 72,000 in 1967. The Korean War, from 1950 to 1953, was the cause of a number of orphaned children. Most of those in the orphanages, however, were not orphaned but abandoned, and their number climbed steadily in the fifteen years after the end of the war. So the problem of homeless children in South Korea was not only a consequence of the war. To most observers, it seemed that it was a consequence of the urbanization and break-up of the extended family attendant upon the growing influence of the West.

Traditional Korea had a family system very much on the Chinese model; the adoption of sons was prescribed for childless families, just as in other Buddhist societies. The much-repeated axiom that 'international adoption is necessary, because the Koreans themselves don't know about adoption' is at best an oversimplification. It is true that relatives were the preferred adoptees, and that boys were preferred to girls. This dovetailed neatly with Western adopters' usual preference for girls, when it came to selecting children for international adoption.

The first orphanages were set up on the Western model by nineteenth-century missionaries. Foreign war relief in 1953 went to the existing institutions, and more were established by charities, mostly Church-based. The families themselves received no relief, and so it came about that: 'In essence, the only way for families to secure help for their children in time of need was to abandon them.'[4]

It is this necessity that has been forced upon poor people by Western social welfare practices ever since the first Poor Laws; it is one of the first and longest-lasting Western exports to the countries that come within the orbit of world capitalism.

Claims that this is only the precursor of an indigenous adoption programme sound hollow when we see how very slowly Korean families have become involved in adoption, and how the number of children exported has continued to grow. The Holt Adoption Programme, one of the pioneers in the overseas adoption of South Korean children, has redoubled its efforts in response to the American and European baby famine.

The Holt Programme was founded by an Oregon fundamentalist who felt impelled by God to do something about the mixed-race abandoned children in Korea in 1953. In 1972, the agency he founded was still placing most of the 2,000 South Korean children a year who found homes overseas. Its present directors believe that the Holt Programme, among others, has led to the development of in-country adoption by Koreans, who now have their own trained social workers. They explain:

> In the emerging countries the new patterns of industrialization break down the extended family system. Yet in the transitional stage, the very mores of blood ties that formerly protected the child now prevent him from being adopted into another home. In other words, the custom of non-related adoption is not yet acceptable.[5]

The American Government passed a Refugee Relief Act in 1953, specifically designed to enable Korean war orphans (many the children of American soldiers) to be adopted by proxy. Proxy adoptions, strongly disapproved of by most adoption agencies, were ended in 1961; but the Holt agency still arranges for children to be placed in their new homes sight unseen, and adopted thereafter.

In its eagerness to place the maximum number of children, Holt has stopped insisting on the religious commitment that its founder saw as indispensable to parenthood. This is perhaps one reason for its success. In South Korea itself, the Church-based agencies have had trouble promoting in-country adoption partly because of their insistence on religious matching: all the children in their care are by definition Christians, but only 10 per cent of the Korean population is.

South Vietnam was the new Korea: during a devastating war, its population was urbanized (a major and deliberate aim of American policy: it makes the population easier to supervise); its family system was all but destroyed, and its city-dwellers were the clients, prostitutes, and servants of the foreign establishment. Yet it tried to resist the wholesale application of inter-country adoption, which would not in any case have been able to solve social problems on this scale.

None the less, such adoption was both popular and fashion-able—Mia Farrow and Jean Kennedy Smith were but two of the much-photographed adopters of baby girls. Black agencies sent delegations to rescue black/Vietnamese children. Holt opened a branch in Saigon. The abandonment problem is entirely reminiscent of Korea, as a fact sheet from AID makes clear:

> Although the children being cared for in orphanages are generally identified as 'orphans', according to the Ministry of Social Welfare more than 50% are neither orphans nor abandoned. They have one or both parents living or close relatives; and in many cases have been placed in orphan-ages because of economic difficulties, or because their families have moved into overcrowded urban areas, or are in movement as refugees or as military dependents.[6]

All the same, there are estimated to be close to a million orphans or half-orphans as a result of the war. Of the probable 25,000 children of mixed Vietnamese/American parentage, 1,000 are in orphanages, as well as 22,000 pure Vietnamese children.

> With rare exceptions, the care of these children is de-plorable. The serious, dangerous overcrowding, parti-cularly in group care for infants, is nothing short of shocking.[7]

126

Some agencies, like the Friends of Children of Vietnam, concentrate their efforts on rescuing the 'dying infant', whose life expectancy is very short because of the lack of care in the orphanages. Some estimates put the mortality rate before the age of 1 year as high as 80 per cent.

However, bureaucracy imposed by both governments made the process of adoption usually very slow. Adopters had to fulfil the requirements of a French-based adoption law (childless, married ten years, one partner over 30, etc) or get a waiver from the President of the Republic. Vietnamese adoption had to be completed before an exit visa was given. A home study of the adopters had to be done by an American agency. Many couples got round these restrictions by pulling strings, or by going to Vietnam and bringing back a baby, but those who adopted through official channels were unlikely to get an infant. And the older child they did get was likely to have a remarkable capacity for survival. The directors of Holt found this to be true in Korea too: 'In our experience, children who have survived particularly grim circumstances frequently show unusual strengths and drives that lead them to excel after adoption.'[8]

Whether the children who need adoption the most are actually the ones selected is a question that has bothered many of the 'donor' governments. Many adopters of Vietnamese children have taken severely deprived and handicapped children, or those with illnesses or war wounds. But some observers believe that the search for so-called adoptable babies has been as intense in Vietnam as anywhere else, and that there is a thriving black market. One relief worker testified before the Senate: 'I think there is very clear evidence that there is the phenomenon of the sale of children in Vietnam for adoption.'[9] Another reported:

> While it is true that a number of adoptions are taking place from Vietnam to Europe and the United States each year, most of these are going through private channels and do not involve social agency participation either at the Vietnam end or in the country of the adoptive parents. As might be expected, a number of bad placements have resulted, including instances where children were placed abroad for adoption without their parents' knowledge or consent.[10]

To the adopters, the issue is crystal clear. They are saving lives, and any government that gets in the way is causing lives to be lost. One couple from Ohio, unable to adopt under the requirements of their home state, flew to Saigon and adopted twins:

> The most discouraging thing was the attitude of the American social service agencies, who could only ask whether the children would be better off in the United States. Our response was that at least in this country there is no war and plenty of food.[11]

The excesses of 'Operation Babylift', the mass evacuation of children just ahead of the advancing North Vietnamese army, exposed the political use to which the war orphans were being put. Observers of all countries were dismayed by the American pretence that conquest by the North would automatically threaten the lives of children. The agencies argued that they were only removing children whose lives were threatened by conditions in the orphanages, and that they had long been negotiating with the South Vietnamese Government for permission to do so. But the revelation that the Thieu regime had decided to release the children in order to curry favour with America brought the entire operation into disrepute.

Of all inter-country adopters the most enthusiastic are the Swedes, who adopted close to 1,500 foreign children in 1972. They are even more certain than the Americans that this is a system wholly advantageous to the children. The Indo-Swedish Society for Child Welfare sends out a glossy folder, *The New Swedes*, showing smiling families of various colour schemes posed among rya rugs and teak bookshelves and modern paintings. The text goes:

> new colour was being added to Sweden's tall, fair, often blond and almost bland homogeneity. Like a strip of chocolate in the Swedish vanilla, the new tots were melting into the picture.

Most of the Swedish children still come from Korea, but countries mentioned as increasingly active donors are 'several countries in Latin America, Liberia, Ethiopia, Iran, Pakistan, India, Thailand, Indonesia, Sri Lanka'. All fit neatly into our map of underdeveloped client states. Children from other European countries are now rare, and fewer than a hundred Swedish children a year are available for adoption—a more compelling argument for the international adopters than the desire to inject a bit of variety into the Swedish colour scheme.

Australia, in effect a suburb of the capitalist metropolis, has the problems of any other developed country after a slight time lag. The movement to organize unmarried mothers is growing; the birth-rate is down, and with it the supply of adoptable babies; there are institutions full of 'children who wait'.

But the burning question in Australia, as in the other countries that sent soldiers to the war in Indo-China, is that of the war waifs fathered by foreign soldiers. It has called into question the 'white Australia' policy (officially abandoned since the Second World War but still behind much government thinking) so successfully that Vietnamese orphans have become the first non-whites to receive assisted immigration.

In 1972, five 'illegal immigrants', South Vietnamese girls between 13 months and 3½ years old, were flown to Sydney and placed with families; the government agreed to allow them to stay. Adopters have attacked the Australian Government for refusing to allow proxy adoptions, which they say would enable interested families to rescue many more children in danger of death. In 1973, six Cambodian children were brought to Australia for adoption. The women who brought them were criticized by World Vision, a charity that cares for children in institutions in their own countries: 'We believe this free-lance operation, which will create great difficulties, should be stopped.'

The women retorted: 'World Vision is putting the pressure on so that only wealthy and religious people will be able to adopt babies. They must realize that if we obey the rules children will die.'[12]

The clash between adopters and government has produced a compromise in which Australia's immigration laws have been relaxed for the children. But to understand the political dimensions of this decision, it is necessary to see it in the historical perspective of Australia's relationship with the rest of South-East Asia. Imported 'Kanaka' labour was sent home at the time of federation, 1901, to avoid giving citizenship to Asians. Australian immigrants from Europe in recent years, fleeing unemployment and bad housing in their own countries, attribute these ills to what they call the race problem. The children of Mediterranean immigrants are often considered hard-to-place, although most European countries would consider them adoptable.

Gunnar Myrdal says of his own Asian studies:

> On the whole, the masses in South Asia in pre-war times were as poor and their lives as miserable as they are now. Their poverty and misery did not, however, induce economists to take any great interest in their stituation ... The cue to the continual reorientation of our work has normally come from the sphere of politics ...[13]

Just as the Cold War stimulated competitive interest in the underdeveloped countries, and therefore serious study of their problems, so demographic change and war guilt over Korea and Vietnam have directed the focus of adoption in the developed countries to new areas. Australian interest in Asian children is more recent than that of the United States, and contrasts even more strongly with earlier attitudes.

In South Vietnam, as in South Korea, one explanation of the need for inter-country adoption has been that it is only an interim solution, and that soon Vietnam, with help from United States advisers, will develop its own adoption and child welfare programmes. We have seen that this is belied by the Korean experience. And now that the chances of its happening in Vietnam have been removed by the communist victory, the American plans have an ironic ring. The Hon. Robert Nooter's testimony before the Senate subcommittee on war relief stated:

> the Vietnamese are deeply concerned that they not embark on social programs so expensive that they cannot be continued after US financial support is withdrawn ... it is important that welfare recipients do not receive benefits in excess of the regular members of society, which would lead to a massive influx of those on the public welfare rolls.[14]

Both of these sound more like American concerns than Vietnamese ones; the second, in particular, indicates that Poor Law thinking was being applied in Vietnam, to do its usual job of ensuring that no one who fell into poverty could escape from it, and that the aid they were given would help to keep them there.

The Governments of the United States, Australia, and the other child-importing countries have been reluctant to get too involved in inter-country adoption, to the chagrin of the potential adoptive parents. This is not so much out of concern for the transplanted children, who by all accounts do perfectly well (although it may be out of concern for the care taken in placement), nor because of worries about the effect of international adoption on the social systems of the donor countries.

One major concern is relations with the Governments of the countries sending the children, which could be damaged by accusations of baby-snatching. A less reputable, but none the less present, concern is to avoid importing large numbers of children seen by the majority in the host country as undesirable, whether racially or in terms of health and fitness. The state agencies claim that they do not have the staff to deal with requests for overseas babies; but the private agencies, whose sources of supply have dried up, have repeatedly offered their services and more often than not been rejected. Another fear of the state is its loss of autonomy if it were to delegate too much power to the voluntary agencies.

Simply discouraging international adoption by inertia, however, is arguably more irresponsible than allowing it to happen. It would be most responsible of all, of course, to obviate the need for it—but it seems that the only countries that have begun to do this are those that have entirely seceded from the capitalist order.

North Korea expresses its disapproval of the south's export of babies in hyperbolic terms:

the traitors of South Korea, old hands at treacheries, are selling thousands, tens of thousands of children going ragged and hungry to foreign marauders under the name of 'adopted children' ... The children of the poor, who are the overwhelming majority of the population, wither away from the very day of their birth, suckling at the dry breasts of their mothers exhausted from hunger and cannot go to hospital in case of illness and they carry boxes instead of satchels and hawk chewing gums and do shoe polishing, exposed to all social maltreatment and humiliation.[15]

Whether or not North Korea has managed to protect all its children from such a fate, an observer reported to the American Senate from North Vietnam, a country still under bomb attack at the time:

> There are virtually no orphans in North Vietnam, because when parents were lost, the child would be adopted by the relative with which the child was living, or adopted by other villagers. So the great problem of orphans we have just heard about in the South is not seen in the North.[16]

Decentralization and strengthening the family system were the North Vietnamese responses to the rigours of war; not only did they present more dispersed and inaccessible bomb targets by this means, they prevented their country from becoming irrevocably dependent on others to look after its children.

Compare this with what one disillusioned I.S.S. worker reports of the Philippines, which have been a showcase of American aid since the Second World War:

> In the Philippines, you can pick up a child in the street. Give the child a chocolate bar, and it will follow you around. Then you go to the embassy and say it is clearly an abandoned child, and you want to adopt it.

Disaster-struck countries are not always as favourable to inter-country adoption as the adopters at first expect them to be. Wild reports of 10,000 unwanted war babies in Bangla Desh raised the hopes of childless couples everywhere. In the event, most of the children were accepted by their families. Only four or five reached England, and not many more went to the United States. The energetic Swedes sent agency representatives who brought out several groups of children: one of the English adopters said: 'The Swedes were there the week before I arrived, and scooped up the lot.'

One Frenchwoman was required by the Biafran Government to return a war orphan she had taken with her to France. And a Catholic foundation in India, that used to send babies for adoption to France, has stopped doing so. In fact, the 1972 Adoption Bill in India is running into opposition, partly because Muslims feel that it would impinge on their personal law, and partly because it contains provision for inter-country adoption. In-country adoption in India is lengthy and difficult, in spite of its long tradition—in a six-month period in 1973, the Indian Council for Child Welfare processed 188 adoptions. A report to 4th N.A.C.A.C. said:

It is estimated that there are between 1·05 million and 1·15 million destitute children in India. Most of these children are not orphaned but abandoned ... Between 1963 and 1970 the Indian Council for Child Welfare helped some 88 children to be placed with foreign nationals. In 1970 a virtual ban on foreign adoptions was imposed. Nevertheless it is known that in Delhi there are several lawyers who, for a substantial fee, offer to procure children and ensure custody.[17]

Often, countries that allow adoption in fact refuse to call it by that name. Foreigners are allowed to take a child out of Colombia, Pakistan, or Libya, for example, 'to assure his education'; they may then apply to adopt under the laws of their own country. An official of the Embassy of Pakistan in London reports:

there is no law on the subject of adoption of children on the Statute Book of Pakistan. Neither is adoption recognized in the personal law of Muslims in Pakistan.
It is understood that 29 Pakistani children were adopted by the nationals of Sweden during the years 1972 and 1973. But this was never an adoption in the strict sense of the term. The Swedes might have got themselves appointed guardians of orphan children under the Guardians and Wards Act, 1890, and then sought permission of the Court to take the child outside the country.[18]

In-country adoption is also difficult in South America, with its Mediterranean-based adoption laws. And minority groups within the population may suffer discrimination as well as the disabilities of life in an underdeveloped country. One woman who adopted two children from Ecuador, by visiting orphanages herself, said:

> There is an adoption law in Ecuador. However, most Indian children who are adopted are unpaid servants. I get rather angry when I hear the argument that children are better off placed in-country. At least from what we know of Ecuador, Indian children are better off not placed in-country.[19]

This raises the questions of international, inter-racial and inter-class adoption all at once. Perhaps one use of inter-country adoption is for the benefit of minority children who are discriminated against in their own countries. This is certainly one of the arguments that has been used about overseas placement of black/Vietnamese children.

International adoption is still only a small fraction of all adoption. and Korea is still the major exporting country.

> Between 1966 and 1972, the number of immigrant orphans to the USA increased by 79%, while the number coming from Asia increased by 141%. Those coming from Korea increased by 241%, and represented over half of the 1972 total of 3,023 ... it would appear that the demand for inter-country adoptions has still to be met, and is controlled only by the decisions of the governments involved.[20]

Naivety about the effect of such placements has decreased as the adopting countries gained more experience. Many of the adopted children, like the children of immigrants, are anxious to assimilate their new culture as fast as possible, and to forget that they ever knew another language or lived anywhere else. Early inter-country adopters clearly did not expect this to happen, as John Adams of Holt reports:

> In the early years some of the parent groups that were formed out of Holt groups were formed with the idea that the children would get to know each other because they

were Korean and as they grew up they could then marry each other.[21]

But all the expertise and good will of the inter-country adopters will go for naught if their efforts are taken to be yet another form of imperialism, which is increasingly how they are seen by many of the countries whose children have been adopted abroad.

It is ironic that as a population crisis looms, a baby shortage should be facing so many countries. It is even more ironic that inter-country adoption cannot help to solve the contradiction. But the growing inequalities between the rich and poor countries seem to be producing a drawbridge mentality in the former and increased nationalism in the latter. No Western liberal today is willing to say that other countries must solve their own problems and care for their own children—but the governments of the Third World are already saying it themselves.

Adoption seems to such countries to be but another form of charity—and like all charity and aid, it is far too small to solve the problem that called it forth. Indeed, there are even indications that it is counter-productive. We have seen how the opening of institutions leads to the abandonment of children; how the injections of aid into countries like South Vietnam has helped to dissolve their traditional social structure. The relationship of aid and charity to adoption becomes even clearer when we consider those advertisements in Western magazines and newspapers, asking people to 'adopt' a foreign child for $10 a month. They show pictures of a small, ragged child, and the headline is 'Kim is hungry', or 'Won't you help?'

The gratification of the contributor is recognized explicitly to be one of the aims of this sort of programme. From the leaflet of the Save the Children Fund:

Children are specially chosen for sponsorship ... Such children are not necessarily the starving or near-destitute ones helped through our welfare centres, but those who will not only be able to derive maximum benefit from the quarterly grants, but also who are most likely to reciprocate the sponsor's interest ... we cannot guarantee the degree of the child's response. Some children are, of course, better correspondents than others.

It goes on to give quotations from the children's letters of gratitude:

My continuing schooling is all owing to your benevolence deeper than the sea and higher than the mountain ...

I am very glad to have found money from you. I think I will go on very well with my subjects at school ... I will try to pass in order to satisfy you.

And all this for £30 a year.

Adopters are, of course, giving more than this. They are giving a considerable part of their lives. And how else are they to contribute anything at all, since it is arguable that donations of money are even less likely to further social change than does inter-country adoption? This is the inescapable argument—and even those who are in favour of more radical solutions cannot deny that in the meantime, other measures are valid.

One such adopter is a radical English journalist, who adopted two children—one South American and one African—he found in the course of his work. Basically, he thinks:

The people who support international adoption are like those who believe in aid to developing countries. They are only trying to do good, and they don't realize that they are actually doing a great deal of harm.

Why, then, did he adopt these children? He believes that any-one faced with the same situation would do as he did—no matter what his views on the ultimate solution to the problem. The moral imperative is clear, as he wryly recognizes: 'I certainly believe that international adoption is just another form of imperialism, but we don't always practise what we preach!'

7 Inter-racial Adoption

The Negro community also has the healthy social custom of attaching no stigma to the illegitimate child and of freely adopting illegitimate children and orphans into established families. A high value is placed on children generally ...

                    Gunnar Myrdal, *An American Dilemma*

In the United States, adoption across class lines often means inter-racial adoption. A disproportionate number of deprived families, more liable than most to breakdown and illegitimacy, are of minority race. The movement to extend adoption to the children who really need substitute families has thus raised all the current questions about integration or separatism.

Until the 1950s, most agencies and individuals rejected outright the notion of inter-racial adoption. It was in fact illegal in many of the southern states, and it was felt that prejudice throughout the country would subject inter-racial families to intolerable strains.

The movement to adopt Korean War orphans cut through some of these assumptions. Exotic children were more acceptable than those of the local minority, and patriotic motives could also be brought into play. Like the movement in England after the First World War, inter-country adoption in the United States had an awakening effect on the domestic scene.

The first breakthrough in the adoption of American minority children came in 1958, when the Child Welfare League of America and the Bureau of Indian Affairs started their Indian Adoption Project. Over the next ten years, 395 Indian children were placed with white adoptive families. In 1968, the project grew into the nationwide Adoption Resource

Exchange and extended its activities to include other groups of children.

There are many reasons why Indian children were chosen for the first trans-racial project. Prejudice against blacks was disseminated throughout the country; anti-Indian feeling was mostly confined to the reservation states. By moving the children to areas where Indians were a rarity, the project could circumvent this feeling. And it was arguable that since Indian children were even more deprived than blacks, they were in the greatest need of imaginative help.

Adoptive parents, too, suffered from the prevailing prejudices, and more were willing to take Indian than black children. Many, in fact, could circumvent their ambivalent feelings about race into a positive acceptance of the idea, by looking at Indians as the first 'real' or 'pure' Americans. Adopting an Indian could add to their status as Americans instead of undermining it in their own eyes.

The overall adjustment of the children in this study is summed up as follows:[1]

excellent: 10%
relatively problem-free: 43%
adequate (strengths outweighing weaknesses): 25%
mixed: 10%
outlook guarded: 10%
outlook dim: 1%
outlook unpromising: 0%

This compares well with the outcome studies of other adoptions; and since it is based on a five-year follow-up, it is expected that its predictive value is high.

There is some correlation in the study between poor adjustment and the parents' initial unwillingness to consider an Indian child; some of the parents did not admit their unwillingness at the time of placement, fearing that it would destroy their only chance of adopting. Many were 'marginal' adopters—parents who, because of their age or the fact that they had children of their own, would not have been considered by the agencies for a white infant. This gives a new angle to some of the recent statistics showing that older parents who already have their own children are more willing to adopt trans-racially: it is not so much a matter of greater willingness as of marginal eligibility. Agencies' statements that this kind of parent is more tolerant, and thus better for a hard-to-place child, begin to sound like rationalizations.

The adopters in this project were no different from the population as a whole politically or intellectually; they were slightly more religious, although there was no correlation between religion and favourable outcome. Most of them indicated that they would not have accepted a part-Negro child for adoption. Usually this was accompanied by a denial of personal prejudice and a statement that it would be too difficult for the child growing up in their community. The 'It's not me who's prejudiced, it's everyone else' echoes the remarks of suburban whites who refuse to sell their houses to blacks.

Many of the couples, at the same time, felt that the social worker they dealt with was more cautious about trans-racial adoption than they were themselves. They concluded by feeling that 'We haven't done anything unusual'.

The somewhat similar British Adoption Project was not initiated in the U.K. until 1965, and it placed only fifty-eight children, although they were more varied racially, including Asian, African, and mixed-race. This project, too, culminated in the establishment of a Resource Exchange. It was preceded by the Hong Kong Project (also administered by International Social Service), which placed about twenty-five Oriental children with British families. Like the American Indian in comparison with the Negro, Orientals were earlier accepted in Britain for trans-racial adoption. Groups that had been the focus of the immigration debate were the last to gain acceptance. The British Adoption Project was even more successful in outcome than the Indian Adoption Project; only three of the children received a doubtful prognosis at the end of a four-year follow-up.

Both these and other studies indicate that adjustment was somewhat better among families lower on the socio-economic scale. Are professional parents too demanding of their children, or are they more ambivalent about adoption? No research has yet answered this question, but it does indicate that modern agency practice is right to give the emotional qualities of a home greater weight than considerations of prosperity, and adds to the validity of subsidized adoption.

These two projects generated a wave of interest in trans-racial adoption, which became increasingly popular during the 'civil rights' years of the 1960s. The Vietnam War broke through the remaining barriers.

In 1971, close to 200 Vietnamese children were adopted in the United States—the first year that international agencies began arranging such adoptions on a large scale. Exoticism and war guilt again operated to make the children highly acceptable. The placements that did break down were probably undermined by the severe physical and emotional handicaps some of the children had suffered in the war. The number of parents applying to their local agencies for these children increased dramatically, and the agencies were finally in a position to say: 'If you want a child of another race, why go all the way to Vietnam to find one?'

In March 1972, the Louisiana law against inter-racial adoption was repealed, and such laws in other states were under attack on constitutional grounds. The next month saw the first blow in the black counter-revolution. The National Association of Black Social Workers, meeting in Nashville, announced its opposition to trans-racial adoption under any circumstances, and claimed that the number of black babies available for adoption reflected the failure of white-dominated agencies to find black adoptive families. Until the agencies hired black social workers who were deeply involved in their own communities, the problem would remain unsolved. In the meantime, black children should not be used to salve the consciences of whites or to fill the gap left by the shortage of white babies. As one well-known black social worker was fond of saying: 'White folks think they can do anything better than anyone else, including raise our children.' The organizations of white inter-racial adopters replied: 'Nobody owns children.' They condemned the 'reverse racism' of the social workers' statement, and the war was on.

The war was being fought not only in the United States but around the world. In September 1971, the first World Conference on Adoption and Foster Placement was held in Milan.

In the chair was Mrs Angie Brooks of Liberia, president of the U.N. General Assembly in 1969 and the adoptive mother of forty-seven children: 'In my heart is love for all mankind, whether it be black, white or Oriental.'

Trans-racial and inter-country placements were the theme of the conference. Margret Ingelstam, the head of Sweden's government adoption agency, explained her country's position:

> We haven't any Swedish children at all for adoption, but we have thousands of childless couples who want to adopt. Other countries show us their trust by sending brown, black and yellow children to pinkish parents.[2]

An anonymous note was sent to the dais: 'Caucasian cultural imperialism is pervading this assembly.' Jane Rowe, director of the Association of British Adoption Agencies, tended to agree. 'Almost we are saying to the developing countries, "You gave us your wealth and you gave us your labour; now give us your children".'

In spite of this kind of international suspicion of adoption across racial and national lines, the growing popularity of inter-country adoption in the United States was accompanied by movements to make inter-racial adoption easier. The issues were not entirely the same: nationalist governments could not intervene, and there was no need to fill the requirements of another country's adoption law. Black spokesmen were increasingly vocal about their opposition to inter-racial adoption, but the placement agencies were faced with large numbers of black children in care, and they were eager to find solutions to the problem. During the 1950s and 1960s, inter-racial adoption gained ground because it was a response to some overwhelming facts.

> In 1965, more than 57 per cent of all children born out of wedlock were nonwhite; but only 9 per cent of the total number of unrelated adoptions were of nonwhite children ... A C.W.L.A. survey showed that in 1969, for every 100 white children awaiting adoption, there were 116 prospective adoptive homes, whereas for every 100 nonwhite children, there were 39 such homes.[3]

These figures posed acute problems to the social agencies and to potential adopters. One problem was that as the agencies began placing black children, more were relinquished to them. Black social workers had proudly claimed that the adoption statistics were misleading, because black families adopted informally, within the extended family, without benefit of law. This turned out to be, at least to some extent, a practice forced on them by agencies that did not accept the relinquishment of black babies, fearing that they would be unable to place them. There was an unmet need, the dimensions of which became clearer as the means to meet it were found.

Trans-racial adoption was one way of meeting this need, and by the mid-'sixties it had gained enough ground to be termed the 'little revolution' by some social workers.

The Open Door Society was chartered in Montreal in 1962, and branches of this organization and of the Council on Adoptable Children, both groups of parents who had adopted trans-racially, were the most ardent recruiters of other such families. Several studies reported that the trans-racial adopters were far above average educationally and professionally, sought little support from their own families and communities, and were exceptionally independent and secure. Many had graduate degrees; if the wives worked, they entered professions. They preferred old, rambling houses to neat suburban boxes. One researcher who studied such adopters in Montreal concluded: 'If ever a child of mine had to be cared for away from me, I would hope it would be in one of these homes.' The profile of the inter-racial adopter had already changed radically from the first tentative agency experiments with 'marginal' couples.

Often, the parents were far ahead of the social workers in their acceptance of mixed-race children. One reported at a conference:

we came originally to an agency with the idea of adopting a so-called hard to place child, but our social worker said for our first child it would be safer for us to have a 'traditional' child to identify with and it was only by our third child that we could get our worker to the point of what we had originally applied for![4]

142

Other social workers tried some rather audacious experiments. Jane Edwards, the elegant black director of New York's prestigious Spence-Chapin agency, took two black children from New York to Sweden for adoption. The enthusiasm of the Swedes, and the chauvinistic outcry at home, had the gingering-up effect she had hoped for on efforts to place black children.

Although trans-racial adoption was rapidly becoming fashionable, it still had a great deal of prejudice to contend with. One 1970 survey indicated that:

> While 56 per cent of the respondents were willing to adopt Spanish-American children and 52 per cent would take American Indian youngsters, only 2 per cent indicated willingness to adopt children of black parentage.[5]

This finding, however, is possibly even more encouraging than other indices of black acceptance in white America. Blacks asserted that it was the baby famine, and not a diminution of racism, that was causing the wave of trans-racial adoptions; the incidence of intermarriage bears out their view. Part of the black separatist movement was to disapprove of intermarriage too, but here they were not combating a fashionable trend.

The Oregon agency Opportunity began collecting figures on agency placement of black children. Of the black children placed by the agencies reporting to them, 33 per cent went to white families in 1968 and 35 per cent in 1970. In the latter year, black children represented 12 per cent of all adoptions and 12 per cent of non-relative adoptions. This means that trans-racial (black/white) adoptions accounted for 4·2 per cent of all adoptions. Compare this with the statistics on intermarriage:

> Studies made in recent years by Dr. Paul Glick, the Census Bureau's family-statistics expert, have revealed that among major ethnic groups the lines are crossed in only about seven-tenths of one per cent of all marriages, and that one-fifth of such intermarriages occur between blacks and whites.[6]

This gives us a figure of 0·14 per cent to compare with 4·2 per cent.

The much greater acceptability of American Indians is also borne out by the marriage statistics: 'More than one-third of them now marry non-Indians; the number of Indian women married to non-Indians doubled between 1960 and 1970.'[7]

Adoption of black children has rapidly become more acceptable to white families throughout the early 1970s. ARENA estimates that 8 per cent of white adoptive applicants in 1969 would have considered black children, while 19 per cent of the 1971 applicants would do so—these figures are higher than in other studies, perhaps because ARENA is known to be primarily interested in the placement of minority children.

However, trans-racial adoption has become less acceptable to blacks. The social workers' Nashville statement said: 'We have committed ourselves to go back to our communities and work to end this particular form of genocide.' The black response was concentrated on three areas: the hiring and training of black social workers; the founding of black agencies; and the development of new kinds of adoption and fostering programmes, specially tailored to the needs of blacks.

The blacks' most bitter accusation was that white families had only begun being interested in black children when there were no more white children available for adoption; that black children, lumped with 'other hard-to-place—handicapped, retarded, too old', were being treated as second-best.

This accusation was hard to deny, especially for agencies that would give a black child to a 'marginal' family that had no hope of getting a white infant. But the counter-charge could be made that the black interest in placing black children was equally not a response to their needs, but a dog-in-the-manger reaction to trans-racial adoption. The all-black agencies were founded not in the mid-'sixties, when the problem of black children in care became acute, but in the early 'seventies, after trans-racial adoption began to be popular.

In these years of change, many studies were launched to determine why so few black families came forward to adopt the black children in need. Several hypotheses were advanced: that black families, even after achieving middle-class status, were so afraid of losing what they had gained that they would not put themselves in economic jeopardy by starting a family; that white-staffed agencies were seen as racist and unapproachable by blacks; that the white agencies did in fact discriminate, if not overtly, then at least by cultural bias; that the agencies saw black children as unadoptable and did not actively seek homes for them.

The most reliable studies indicated that blacks adopted as often as whites of the same economic status—but that poor blacks, like poor whites, were unwilling to ask for this extra drain on their income—and there were proportionately many more poor blacks than whites. All the signs of poverty were higher among blacks: illegitimacy was much higher, there were more families headed by women (28 per cent in 1971), and there were more families living on assistance. Because of their many economic disadvantages, which were decreasing slowly if at all, blacks had become a 'donor' group as far as adoptable children were concerned; and the same disadvantages prevented them from also being a 'receiving' group. This was the basic problem.

It was a problem analysed in considerable depth by many of the blacks who created the movement against trans-racial adoption. Ben Finley, who founded Chicago's Afro-American Family and Community Services in the wake of the riots following the murder of Martin Luther King, pointed out that the American child welfare tradition was the heir of the English Poor Laws. Its central principle was that the indigent must be punished. He pointed out that foster mothers receive two or three times as much money as mothers living on Aid to Families with Dependent Children (A.F.D.C.)—a statistic that obviously has a great deal to do with the relinquishing of children for adoption. The crowning irony in his eyes was that white people had throughout the history of the United States used black people to raise their children—now they were denying them the opportunity of raising their own.

Most of these observations were made at a series of Black Child Advocacy Conferences, held in major cities during 1972 by the Black Child Development Institute (B.C.D.I.). Another spokesman at these conferences, Dr Basil Matthews, developed the same theme.

To black people black child adoption is essentially a concern for well-being, not for welfare. Well-being and welfare

are not the same thing. Well-being is a creative urge and is positive. This is the African heritage. Welfare at its best is a negative thrust. It is an attempt to rehabilitate on a care and maintenance basis segments of the population whom the Protestant ethnic capitalist society has already damaged or destroyed and whom the system, by its very nature, is committed to damaging and destroying.[8]

Alfred Herbert, the director of B.C.D.I., puts his case with tact and charm, but he takes an uncompromising line. He describes the organization's function as seeking the social causes of the disabilities suffered by black children instead of simply analysing their pathology. To Herbert, the strong extended family and the woman-centred family are part of the African heritage of American blacks, not, as has often been claimed, the legacy of slavery. A speaker at the Boston conference (a city where as many as 45 per cent of black children adopted went to white families) quoted a letter from a former student:

> after a lecture from a speaker on how Black families do not adopt, one student stood up and stated that many Blacks do adopt but not through traditional channels. This student gave an account of how he and his sister were raised by a cousin. Another got up and related a similar story, then another, then another until over half of the students related stories of how they knew of, or were participants in an informal adoption. The group represented the northern and southern United States, the Caribbean and Africa.[9]

To these speakers, it seemed that the traditional black ways of caring for children had been disrupted by the move to the northern cities (immigration and urbanization, the two persistent themes again); by the punitive welfare system combined with unemployment, which meant that the best thing an unemployed black man could do for his family was to leave them, so that the wife could collect A.F.D.C.; and by the tendency of the authorities to take children into care, rather than to use the same money to keep the family together. But the main enemy at the moment seemed to be the trans-racial adopters.

If you don't move into the Black community, some other people will move; the Open Door Society, Families for Inter-Racial Adoption or Council on Adoptable Children, for example. These are the white families who are making the decision that they can parent Black children.[10]

The white families thus identified claimed that the situation was more complicated than that. Was growing up in an institution preferable to a white home? What about children who were half-white anyway? To the latter question the blacks had an unqualified answer.

There are no trans-racial or bi-racial children. It is a disservice to these children to consider them to be anything except what the community considers them, and that is Black children.[11]

They quoted Mahalia Jackson: 'Black blood is like the blood of Jesus, one drop makes you whole.'

This brings us to what the blacks saw as the crux of the whole matter: the question of identity. How could a white family prepare a black child to face discrimination, and teach him the subtle coping mechanisms that black parents transmit to their children? Who would he identify with as an adult?

All the outcome studies that have been done so far cannot answer these questions, because the children are still too young. How many of the children will marry blacks? Will the mixed-race children raised by white families be defined as black or white by society? Will they be integrationists or separatists?

In part, it is impossible to answer these questions because it is impossible to say what being black will mean in America in the 1980s. In the last decade, the number of black professionals has doubled and that of black servants has been halved. The black illegitimacy rate is beginning to fall (although Alfred Herbert asks: 'Is illegitimacy the right word, now that it is so acceptable?'). Black income is rising rapidly, although it is not closing the gap separating it from white income. Legislation and challenges in the courts have had a great effect on blacks' admission to universities and jobs. There are signs of a move back to the inner cities by whites anxious to escape the sterile suburbs—this may improve the tax famine that has made city rehabilitation difficult.

All these things are making it slightly easier to be black, and there are already indications that the era of 'black pride' is giving way to one of black confidence. White families who have adopted black children are sure that their confidence will be increased by the knowledge that at least some white people can be loved and trusted.

This certainty is shared by those who have observed these families in action. A study done for the U.S. Children's Bureau found that:

> Those who spoke from direct experience or observation came out two to one in favor of cross-racial adoptions. Those who based their views on hearsay or on principle—chiefly the community representatives—were a little more often opposed than in favor.[12]

Many black social workers remain unconvinced by these arguments. They point out that instead of insisting on formal adoption, which might necessitate trans-racial placement for some children, less secure but more practical alternatives can be found among blacks. A representative of a New York agency that uses long-term foster placement explains this point of view:

> the staff feels that we should leave them in foster homes where they feel very definitely the foster parents will rear them to maturity whether or not they adopt them. Their position, and these are young black staff members, is that your statement on criteria may not be their statement on criteria. I would rather keep them in a black foster home than place them in a white adoption home. I don't think permanence is more important than black identity.[13]

Some black spokesmen have gone even further than this, and indicated that they see community-based institutions as preferable to trans-racial adoption. But the black experience with children's institutions has been so damaging that this view has few adherents, at least without a radical re-thinking of the staffing, organization, and location of the homes.

Suspicion of adoption agencies is definitely part of the black rejection of trans-racial adoptions. Some say that white social workers feel more comfortable with white families, and thus think of trans-racial adoption as the easiest way to place black children. The agencies have signally failed to serve the black community—first by turning away black children on the grounds that they were hard to place, then by turning away black adopters on the grounds that they were not middle-class enough. The insistence on agency placement is also attacked by some blacks, who say that attempts to outlaw third-party or direct placements are an attack on black families: 'You cannot have any law that will stop it, it is part of our culture, it is part of our heritage, it is part of our function, it is part of our being.' This was said at the New Orleans Black Child Advocacy Adoption Conference by a director of Homes for Black Children, the Detroit agency that has been one of the most successful at recruiting black adopters, largely because it is an agency entirely founded and staffed by black people.

Both white and black agencies have attempted to solve the whole controversy by finding enough black homes for all the black children who need families. The history of this effort is an illustration of how very malleable are agency requirements and practices in the face of a crisis.

That there is a crisis in the numbers of black children in care is undeniable. The number of black children now in institutions is estimated to be as high as 80,000, and the prediction is that greater success in placement will be followed, at least in the short term, by a rise in the numbers relinquished to agencies.

One of the earliest crisis programmes was launched by the Children's Aid Society of Pennsylvania in 1964, when a back-up of babies in the Philadelphia city hospital forced them to act quickly: 'The situation came to a head because mothers, unable to care for their newborns, left them behind in the safe hands of the hospital.'[14] With the help of past adopters, a large number of black families was quickly located and studied by the agency, and the babies were placed immediately. The agency called it a 'quasi-adoption program' because financial support from the agency was continued until the completion of legal adoption, usually several months later. This meant that many of the obstacles that discouraged black adopters were removed.

There were not the usual long delays before and after the home study, and a final decision about adoption was not demanded of the parents until the child had been with them for a while. The agency, however, had to see that the parents fulfilled the usual requirements for adopters, some of which were part of the law, and their recounting of this part of the story indicates some of the reasons why black families might resent investigation by white social workers:

> Some of those who were accepted had tasks to accomplish before placement. For example, some couples were assisted in accomplishing a legal marriage. Others were helped to investigate old police and prison records and to work through feelings that remained.[15]

Still, there were many things about the programme that went against traditional notions of good social work practice.

> The parents in the quasi-adoption program were older, were less secure economically, and had less education and fewer job skills. The children placed with them, as compared with those placed in traditional adoption homes, had had more foster home placements, longer stays in institutions and shelters during infancy, more abuse and more neglect.[16]

None the less, a follow-up study about four years later detected no psychological differences in functioning between the quasi-adoption families and a control group of traditional adoptive families. Marginal families who might well have been rejected by the agency in normal circumstances made just as good parents as those selected by the usual methods.

'Quasi-adoption' was one of the programmes that launched the notion of financial support for adopters who had all the emotional qualities but few of the material ones. This idea has broadened into subsidized adoption, now legal in most of the states of the United States, which has proved one of the agencies' most useful tools in reaching black adopters.

To be politically acceptable, subsidized adoption had to be firmly restricted to children for whom non-subsidized adopters were unlikely to be found. In practice, this has usually meant long-term foster parents who wanted the security of adoption, but could not afford to dispense entirely with the foster-care stipend. Institutional care is more expensive than foster care, and foster care is more expensive than subsidized adoption — this has been the argument in its favour. The parents trade a certain proportion of their foster-care income for the security of adoption, as a report to the Illinois General Assembly made clear:

> The subsidy agreement worked out with Mr and Mrs Morris, enabling them to adopt the twins, calls for the Department to provide a $75 monthly subsidy per child instead of the $115 per month per child boarding care fee ... The dollar savings to the State of Illinois over the next 13 years is estimated at $12,120.[17]

Subsidized adoption has helped with the placement of children likely to need expensive medical care or psychiatric treatment; it is increasingly being used to attract poor families to the idea of adoption, and in many areas of the country this means black families.

Subsidy is only one aspect of the search for black parents, because poverty is only one of the things that kept them away from the agencies. Trudy Bradley Festinger has done two major studies of the relationship of black families and adoption agencies. In 1967, she found that although most of the children awaiting adoption were black, more black families than white were rejected by the agencies, and more black families that had been considered suitable withdrew after the initial contact.[18] In 1972, she compared whites and blacks who withdrew from the adoption process after an initial agency contact. The reasons given more often by whites than by blacks were:

> Pregnancy
> Independent adoption
> Preference for other agency
> Social worker

The reasons given more often by blacks were:

Financial
Agency rules and procedures
Miscommunication[19]

Obviously, the whites were adept at 'shopping around' for a baby when faced with agency delays; the blacks tended to be discouraged from adopting at all. Special efforts to recruit black families did not necessarily make things better: many observed that the agency started out by making things sound easy, but nothing followed except delays and 'snooping'. Many would have liked to talk to parents who had already adopted — they did not want to ask questions of the social worker who was judging them. Two especially interesting findings emerged from this study: 60 per cent of the black wives believed that one needed a large bank account to adopt (although this was denied by the agencies); and fewer families withdrew after contact with a black social worker.

Black agencies staffed by black social workers have, in keeping with this finding, been the most successful at recruiting black adopters—sometimes by methods that are directly contrary to those used by white agencies. As a director of Homes for Black Children says:

> working the normal 9 to 5 day is not part of a successful adoption agency in the Black community: you don't ask a Black man to miss going to work to come in for an interview, we say that we will come to his home.[20]

The agency must also make a special effort to obtain the legal documents required by the adoption process—for example, southern blacks may not have birth certificates if they were born in a state that did not keep such records on blacks at the time. These are two examples of areas that white agencies often use as tests of an applicant's sincerity. Extra efforts on the part of adopters to come to meetings with the social worker, even if it means missing work, and to be prompt about supplying the requisite documents, show that the couple really want to adopt and have no ambivalence. It is idle to cling to these requirements where they are not appropriate: for instance, in the case of a black man who may be paid by the hour.

Another method of recruiting black families was pioneered by Spence-Chapin—foster placement with a view to adoption. It was easier to recruit foster families than adoptive ones, and it was not necessary to wait for a final decision by a mother who was not sure she wanted to give up her child. However, the agency went ahead with placing the children, with seeking termination of parental rights after the legal period had elapsed, and with applying for subsidized adoption. About half of the children fostered in this programme have since been adopted— an extraordinarily high rate.

Spence-Chapin now places all the black infants relinquished to it, but because it was not reaching enough of the people who needed it, it started a Harlem agency, Harlem-Dowling, in 1969. Jane Edwards describes its success:

> Harlem-Dowling is there to reach the community, the unwed mothers who would never go downtown. We went up and down the streets and told people about the agency; we got the locals to talk about it; we hired paraprofessionals from the area. We work closely with the mothers, and we're part of a complete social service.[21]

The Harlem-Dowling motto for adopters is 'screen in, not out'. Few families are rejected. But far from being primarily interested in releasing babies for adoption, the agency is also engaged in helping the unmarried mother if she wants to keep her child. Jane Edwards says of her work at Spence-Chapin, 'I do some inter-racial placements and I don't care who knows it,' but Harlem-Dowling finds its adopters within the black community.

Another study of agencies' response to black adopters came up with many of the same conclusions, and with a further one: 'current contact with the social work profession by agency social workers ... is negatively associated with placement of black children with black adopters.'[22] In other words, the risks inherent in placement with black adopters—their timidity in approaching the agency, their sometimes shaky financial status, the fact that many of the wives worked—were seen by the more 'professional' social workers as obstacles to adoption. Their professionalism implied minimizing the risks as much as possible, even though there was no evidence that what they saw as risks actually jeopardized the success of a placement.

The white agencies that had trouble recruiting black adopters began gradually to re-evaluate their methods. Some, like the Children's Home Society of New Jersey, set up a black agency-within-an-agency. Their Advisory Committee on Black Adoptions, largely staffed by black social workers, evolved a list of criteria for agencies to use in dealing with black families.

> fee scale can be waived
> no strict requirements
> mother does not have to stop work
> home ownership not a must
> no set income
> may have other children
> no age limit
> single applicants accepted
> no set length of marriage
> no fertility test required
> study begun immediately

One interesting thing about this list is that nothing on it has ever been shown to affect adoption outcome unfavourably, but every item has at one time or another been used by agencies to weed out applicants. The movement for black adoption has forced a much-needed re-examination of the criteria for all adoptions. There are other requirements, too, like living within the area served by the agency and attending church, that are related to the supply-and-demand situation rather than to adoption outcome, and that agencies have jettisoned when dealing with black children.

The C.W.L.A.'s Standards for Adoption Service have reflected the vagaries of racial pressure. As Florence Kreech reports:

In 1959 the Child Welfare League's Adoption Standards strongly urged that children be placed in homes of their own race. A few years later the N.A.A.C.P. and the Urban League objected to the 1959 position and urged consideration of interracial adoptions. When the League's Adoption

Standards Committee further reviewed this question, it found that the possibility of adoptive placement for black children was limited because of a shortage of homes. In the 1968 revised adoption standards the committee took a more positive position with regard to transracial placements.[23]

The Adoption Standards are now sent out with a 1973 supplement, which says:

In today's social climate, other things being equal, we believe it is preferable to place children in families of their racial background. We, however, reaffirm transracial adoption as one means of achieving needed permanence for some children. Children should not have adoption denied or significantly delayed when adoptive parents of other races are available.

'Other things being equal' is perhaps the only phrase in this statement that would bring an ironic smile from a black militant.

One of the most highly politicized areas of inter-racial adoption is the question of Vietnamese children with black American fathers. Half of the American-fathered children in orphanages are black/Vietnamese, and the Interagency Vietnam Adoption Committee was started by some black agencies to ensure that they did not go to white American adopters. It was predicted that because of their racial difference, these children would be as unacceptable to their own society as were the children of French Senegalese soldiers. However, a fact-finding expedition estimated that no more than 500 black/Vietnamese children were in orphanages awaiting adoption. It seemed to the black agencies that this number of black families could easily be found, and that they could best be found through black agencies. In 1973, the Agency for International Development (AID) stated that: 'the Black community would not be prepared to service the agencies operating in Vietnam unless a major voice in policy at all levels was assured.'[24]

In the wake of this kind of thinking, some people predicted that there would be only one generation of children adopted trans-racially, and that the 'little revolution' was already over.

155

But although black infants were no longer waiting for adoption in many parts of the country, nor going to white families, there was still a large number of older black children in institutions, and family breakdown causing such children to be taken into care was continuing at least at the same rate.

The supply of black adopters was not sufficient to meet the need, especially, as one social worker put it, 'because of the recession that Nixon says isn't happening'. Most people continued to see trans-racial adoption as at least an interim solution to the problem. Both black and white social workers agreed on some of the characteristics to look for in such adopters, and one cardinal item was previous involvement with black people. As Mrs Sadie Wheeler, the motherly and militant black 'adoption lady' at the D.C. Department of Human Resources, observed:

> With trans-racial applications, we ask: 'What's your exposure to that group?' Do they see a need for continued racial identification for the child? You know on that phone when you're talking to a do-gooder. There was a rash of calls a couple of years ago, whites wanting black children … one woman said it would really fix her mother-in-law if she adopted a black child. Well, I always ask them if they know any black people, and sometimes they say, 'Oh yes, there are black families all around us—Mrs. Smith's housekeeper is black, and there's that family on the corner, the landlord hasn't been able to get them out yet, well, they're black …'[25]

Arlene Nash of ARENA also had doubts about some of the transracial families she saw.

> They could be the best parents in the world, and still have an identity crisis on their hands. How will the child feel about his own background? I know parents who adopted Korean children who are buying Korean cookbooks, all that bit … Some of them really want a racial assortment. They write articles about it, and hold groups—I sometimes wonder when they spend time with the children.[26]

These accusations would seem highly unfair to most trans-racial adopters, who quickly stop thinking of themselves as belonging to that class at all — they are simply people raising their children just like anyone else.

The American debate about trans-racial adoption is an intensified local version of the controversy over international adoption. American blacks have been able to launch a more sustained self-help campaign than many other satellite groups, because they are better-organized and better-off, but the argument is the same. No one seriously doubts the capacity for love or the humanitarian motives of the adopters; all that is in doubt is the political issue of who the children belong to.

Erik Erikson, in a conversation with Huey Newton, said:

> There is a religious element to all true transvaluation of values, especially where it concerns a faith in the God-given gifts of an exile or suppressed people. One might even say that a responsible religious attitude is impossible where one has not first learned to believe in the genius of the people one happens to emerge from: the acceptance of foreign gods whose business it is to favor other skin colors can only lead to a religiosity of meekness and self-debasement.[27]

To a black militant, this is the crux of the matter: how can an oppressed race gain its identity if 'advantage' is defined for a child of that race as becoming a member of a family of the dominant race? Busing black children to white schools, integration marches to white suburbs, inter-racial adoption—the implication always seems to be that for a black, success is defined as admission to the white world.

The continuing definition of black children—in common with crippled, retarded, and delinquent children—as hard-to-place is part of the issue; so is the debate about the intellectual capacity of blacks. Will the interests of the black child be best served by placing him in a white family, and thus further demeaning his race, or by affirming the capacity of his race to bring up children well by placing him with black adopters? The token nature of trans-racial adoption, no matter how good the adopters, is its insuperable flaw in the eyes of blacks.

Inter-racial adoption in the United States, however, at least concerns two groups who have been part of the same society for 300 years. Everyone understands the rules of the game, even if they sometimes see themselves as opponents.

In Britain, inter-racial adoption often means inter-cultural or inter-country adoption as well, and is altogether a more complex matter. It has met little opposition from minority groups, because they are smaller and less well-organized than American blacks, but the feelings on both sides are beginning to be the same.

One of the first trans-racial adopters in Britain, who has three children of her own and three mixed-race adopted children, explained how she started out more than twenty years ago:

> We first thought of adopting coloured children because we minded about racialism, and it seemed a good way to do something about it. None of the agencies wanted to know — they were all frightened of making a mistake. We started with the National Children, Barnardo's, all the big ones — the local authorities weren't doing adoption then. Barnardo's said 'We would never contemplate adoption for a coloured child—they are always the most difficult children in the nursery.' Finally the Moral Welfare people (Church of England) agreed to help us …

Because she was treading new ground, this woman was allowed to set her own rules; she adopted two children so close in age to two of her own that they grew up as sets of twins. The family always lived in neighbourhoods where there were no other black children: 'No prejudice had got started in these areas, and the children felt a bit special being the only ones of another race.'

The opposite tack was taken by a recent inter-country adopter, who purposely lives in a very heterogeneous neighbourhood in London:

> I wondered whether it was wrong of me to keep Shiva's original name, but then I was collecting the kids from school and all their friends were named Ali and Spiros and Mustapha, and I thought really it doesn't make any difference.

There are 30,000 children in institutions in Britain, another 30,000 in foster care, and 11,000 in private fostering arrangements. One-fifth of the institutionalized children are black or mixed-race, and the proportion rises to an estimated four-fifths when it comes to private fostering. Many of the black girls who relinquish babies for adoption are now requesting that the child go to a black family, so the Adoption Resource Exchange are mounting a drive to find black adopters.

But perhaps the most vexed question in this whole area is confusion about the role of adoption as opposed to fostering, and what both concepts signify to people who come from a tradition of kinship fostering.

As we have seen, kinship fostering compensates for separation from the mother by providing an extended family network that never entirely severs the original bond with the parents. Mothering is divided up among several people, including the natural mother, even if it is the grandmother or aunt who provides most of the child's day-to-day care.

This kind of system often breaks down entirely when part of the family emigrates to Britain, or returns to Africa or the West Indies after several years in the U.K. And it breaks down without the people who are doing it being aware at first that it is not working.

The Coram Foundation sees many cases of this kind, and their adoption officer tells of an African father who sought a long-term foster family for his child, saying 'I want my child brought up in an English home — the very best, like my training.' This kind of thinking is, naturally enough, shared by the English — who, if they are imbued with current child-welfare thinking, may then be reluctant to return the child to its parents.

The newspapers recently reported the case of a 5-year-old Nigerian girl who had been with foster parents since the age of 4 months, and whose mother was refused permission to take her back to Nigeria. In deciding that the girl should stay with her (white) foster parents, Lord Justice Davies said: 'the decisive factor in allowing the foster parents' appeal was that Eve, apart from blood and colour, was an English girl.'

159

was comforted by a welfare officer from the Nigerian High Commission, who said: 'This judgment will be a lesson to all African people in England on the question of fostering. Black people who seek English foster parents should be warned of the danger of losing their children.'[28]

This is a situation in which current opinion about the 'best interests of the child' comes face to face with accusations of racism and cultural bias.

The Commonwealth Students' Children Society, founded by a Ghanaian, finds several hundred foster parents each year for the children of Africans and West Indians studying in London. When both parents are in school or working, the lack of day care and, usually, of living space (80 per cent are in one-room flats) mean that the child must go to a foster-parent. A social worker for the Society was asked why so many chose unsupervized private fostering arrangements, rather than going to the local authority.

> Because of discrimination ... By that I mean cultural rather than racial discrimination. The African's first priority is to get an education in England, not to sit at home looking after the children. But the English social worker can't understand it. The African mother sees no social stigma in fostering. It's a temporary *sharing* of the same child. But the social worker makes a moral judgment. He believes that this is a bad example of motherhood. So there's tremendous tension there ... 'Why can't she wait until her children are at school before she does her studying? *I* had to', is a comment I often hear.[29]

Is it in fact a bad example of motherhood? The African mother can point to a cultural tradition in which children have been fostered for hundreds of years without emotional damage. But new situations create new stresses, and the occasional investigations into private fostering indicate that most of the children cared for in this way are not receiving adequate care. The separation of families, when this is a cultural as well as a physical separation, can have terrible effects.

A recent study of teenage suicide attempts admitted to

Birmingham General Hospital revealed three clearly defined groups. One was made up of West Indian immigrants who had, in the words of the doctor who made the study, 'a strikingly similar background'.

> In each instance the child had been left behind in the West Indies, usually with grandparents, and joined the family in England years later. But by that time these family units were quite different and these children just didn't fit in.[30]

Another instance in which upholding the rights of foster parents (and, according to child welfare thinking, the best interests of the child) could have led to accusations of racism was the Parks case, in which a $4\frac{1}{2}$-year-old Indian boy was returned to his father, who had voluntarily put him into foster care, kept up contact, and always declared his intention of having him back. The newspapers reported,

> From one of the more comfortable suburbs of Nottingham he has suddenly been plunged into one of the poorest. From a white Anglo-Saxon home and community he has been thrust into an unknown Indian community. From a family where mother was always at home he joins a family where there is no mother, a 65-year-old father who speaks little English, and a 14-year-old sister who runs the house ...[31]

But the boy's widowed father, faced with the necessity of supporting four children, decided on quite reasonable grounds that the two youngest would be better off in foster care until they started school. The child undoubtedly runs a high risk of emotional damage through the changes of care to which he has been subjected; but it is obviously no fault of the father that he is poor, widowed, and faced with the unpleasant necessity of committing his children to the care of others.

Court decisions like this and the case of Eve show that there is no easy and universal solution to the question. The law is trying to keep an uneasy balance among the claims of the various parties, often with results that please no one.

At the moment, foster parents are seeking greater rights over the child they may have fostered for several years, and the indications in England are that they will get these rights. Long-term fostering as practised in traditional societies seems to have almost no place amid the alienation of a modern city, and to provide sufficient security for the children, it must gradually merge into adoption.

This will be difficult to accept for people who have practised such fostering, as it has been difficult for American blacks to accept. But it is the professional consensus that greater continuity for the child must be achieved even at the expense of greater hardship for the parents. Poverty, homelessness, the necessity of earning a living—all such reasonable excuses do not alleviate the consequences for the child of broken relationships in the early years. But to the many other penalties of belonging to a 'satellite' group is being added the risk of losing one's children.

People who disagree with this consensus seemingly have no means of preventing its consequences, once they are caught up in the system. In spite of black lobbying against trans-racial placement, new weapons are being discovered and used by whites who would rather adopt black children than see them grow up in institutions.

The American 'non-discrimination' law has recently been used by whites who claim that they are being told by adoption agencies that only applications from blacks are being accepted, as they have only black children available for adoption. One couple challenged such a policy in Ohio, and the District Court issued an order that the Montgomery County Children's Service

1. must accept applications for adoption from people of any race who are seeking to adopt a child of a different race.
2. must process these applications in a normal manner.
3. cannot determine that a child is unavailable for adoption because of his race or the race of any prospective parents eligible to adopt the child.

This was an inevitable development, and it has implications

not only for trans-racial adoption. Similar cases have been brought over the age of adoptive applicants, as well as over the question of religion. It is part of a movement by citizens' groups to hold the agencies publicly accountable for their policies and practices, and to challenge those that seem to raise a question of civil rights.

Black social workers have, however, made the claim that the spectre of trans-racial adoption is frightening black parents away from the agencies they were just beginning to trust. The latest C.W.L.A. figures show an 11 per cent decline in the numbers of black children released to the public agencies; is this a confirmation of the social workers' claim? Other agencies report that the supply of black adoptive parents is showing the effects of the coming depression, and that, for the immediate future at least, trans-racial adoption will continue to be necessary.

The twists and turns of this argument will continue to follow the state of race relations in the whole of society.

8 The Adopters

Who adopts, and why?

In most societies, it has been the childless or the relatively childless — those who could not have as many children as they wanted, or who had only daughters when they wanted a son. It has also been step-parents, or single mothers making their children legitimate. In the West, in fact, about half of all adoptions occur between relatives.

A concise profile of adoption in the United States was drawn in Arizona in 1962:

> Big business and professional men adopted children only when they were unable to bear children of their own. Social agencies supplied them with illegitimate children of unrelated persons. Lower-middle-class adoptions more commonly involved adoption by the husband of children born to his wife in a previous marriage ... At the bottom of the social scale, unskilled workers, farm laborers, and unemployed men frequently adopted children who were distantly related to them but whose parents were unable to care for them.[1]

This typology is still basically accurate, but the shortage of adoptable illegitimate babies has meant that the first category is becoming interested in other groups of children, and that the informally adopted children of the last category are now acceptable for placement by the social agencies.

In addition, there is one entirely new class of adopters: those who choose to adopt although they are able to have as many children as they want. The motives of this group are under increasing scrutiny, since they are the people agencies are coming to consider most appropriate for hard-to-place children. Their reasons for adopting range across a broad spectrum, from piety to war guilt to fears about overpopulation. Some of the social stigma that used to be attached to childlessness is now coming to surround those who bear more than their replacement quota of two children. They are urged to adopt the rest.

Adopters who are not automatically attracted to the idea because of childlessness often need energetic recruitment. Once they adopt, however, they become ardent recruiters themselves. Unlike traditional adopters, who want to forget the fact of adoption as quickly as possible and be like any other family, many of the new sort pride themselves on their 'difference'.

These two groups are not mutually exclusive. In spite of professional doubts about whether it will work, many childless couples have become complex adopters, although it often takes a period of introspection before they can relinquish the narcissistic satisfactions of adopting an infant like the one they might have had.

Even among the childless population, adoption is by no means an automatic response. One English study showed that not more than one in every four childless couples decides to adopt, and that the determining factor seems to be the wife's relationship with her own parents.[2] A woman who had a happy childhood, and who believed that her own mother enjoyed the experience of motherhood, was more likely to seek the same experience herself.

This and other studies report that the childless felt little sense of relief and unexpected freedom—emotions attributed to them by others. On the contrary, they felt foolish and set apart by their relative leisure and affluence, and that all their compensations—pets, vacations—were considered comical by the rest of the world.

Estimates of 10 to 15 per cent are usually given for the incidence of infertility in Western populations; but as Myrdal points out, it is notoriously difficult to arrive at an accurate figure:

The subject of human fecundity is one of the least known areas of demography. It is difficult to assess because the production of offspring, which is the only absolute evidence of fecundity, normally falls well below the biological potential in any population.[3]

In other words, it is impossible to sort out voluntary from involuntary infertility simply on the basis of statistics, and almost impossible to determine whether a particular group is postponing pregnancy or desperately attempting to achieve it.

The accusation of self-indulgence levelled at childless couples is hard to bear if they are in fact trying to have children; just as maddening is the widely held view that infertility is psychosomatic — an idea thought to be proven by the very unscientific evidence that everyone seems to know someone who has conceived after adopting.

Students of this question now believe that the myth has some truth, but only in certain circumstances. Samples of women with no organic cause of infertility, still young enough to be maximally fertile, do show a slightly increased incidence of conception after adopting — although visiting a fertility clinic often has the same effect even before treatment is undergone, as does simply registering with an adoption society. Perhaps, the observers conclude, adoption simply hastens an event that would have occurred in any case.

Recent work is beginning to indicate that there is a close relationship between stress and infertility, and that stress is cumulative. That is, the tense and neurotic personality already has one strike against it. Sedentary, competitive work and modern urban life are other sources of stress. Together, they can increase the infertility rate of a population.

Periods of decreased birth-rate are usually explained by social and economic factors. But do people deliberately choose to have fewer children in times of economic uncertainty, or is the added stress enough to make conception more difficult? The birth-rate in England is now (1975) the lowest ever recorded, and it is falling almost as fast in most Western countries. But the desire to adopt does not appear to have slackened. Perhaps this anomaly can be partly explained by the stress theory.

Adopters who have already had children are insulated against some of the emotional difficulties faced by the previously childless. Anxiety is alleviated by experience; the barrage of feelings experienced by the first-time adopter who is also a first-time parent is avoided.

Infertile adopters, once they negotiate all the hurdles and obtain a child, are faced with the necessity of finding an attitude to take towards the whole experience: a task in which they are given little help by those around them. Just as they are trying to accept the child, they have to persuade relatives, neighbours, and friends to accept him too.

They are not helped by the knowledge that nowadays the adopted child's emotional difficulties are attributed to his parents' ambivalence about adoption. As one pioneer study put it:

> Adopted children, even if adopted at an early age, seem more prone to emotional disturbances and personality disorders than non-adopted children. This was found to be the case even when they had not experienced psychological trauma before adoption.
>
> These findings were hard to explain in terms merely of the child's awareness of being adopted. The author suggests that a more likely interpretation can be found in terms of the adoptive parent's or parents' unconscious and unresolved aversion towards parenthood.[4]

The extra motivation towards parenthood may not by itself be enough to overcome this underlying aversion attributed to childless adopters, and, according to one social worker, this is one reason why adopting a second baby can be even more difficult than the first:

> With the first child, she thinks, 'Look at me, getting up in the night like everyone else!' She's thrilled and very maternal. Then maybe with the second child, she can't bring herself even to cuddle it; she just can't think of it as hers.

New hypotheses are constantly being developed about what makes adoption difficult. The new parents and their relatives used to watch anxiously for signs of hereditary problems, whether physical or emotional. Then the pendulum swung to

167

environment, and the anxious adopters themselves felt guilty about their children's hostility or aggression or immaturity.

There is some evidence that this phase too is coming to an end. But this time, the swing is not back to heredity (at least not in the same way), but to the child's early behaviour and whatever it is that determines temperament.

The American behaviourists have been criticized for looking at the child as a blank slate, to be written on at will by its trainers. Recent experiments have concentrated on the socializing of the child as a process of interaction, that begins with certain established patterns on both sides, and proceeds by the mutual modification of behaviour.

Studies of babies' cries have shown that they often reveal physical or mental abnormalities. The mother who responds with coldness, hostility, or even violence to her child's cry may therefore have had these reactions elicited by the baby itself. Newborns vary enormously in such things as levels of irritability, muscular tension, and length of crying periods. The mother's instinctual maternal behaviour is in large part elicited by the baby's behaviour, and if his genetic programming is abnormal the nurturing relationship may be impaired.

A mother who is separated from her baby for the first few days of life—perhaps to recover from a difficult delivery—has much more difficulty responding to his signals later on. The rapport between mother and child has suffered a setback that may show itself in increased crying by the baby and nervous tension in the mother. It is not, therefore, surprising that it often takes adoptive mothers some time to overcome the effects of a similar setback. Instead of beginning with a certain knowledge of each other's physical and emotional responses, the new parent and child have to begin by making a temperamental adjustment that may be anything but easy.

In a way, this makes it easier to acknowledge the different tasks ahead of the adoptive parent. Instead of asking 'Is the parent to blame, because of his negative response to adoption?' future research will ask 'What causes negative interaction, and how can the parent–child relationship be set on a smoother course?'

There are some sociological differences between adoptive parents that seem to affect their performance as much as behavioural differences. Kirk has speculated that the usual Western preference for adopting girls indicates ambivalence about adoption, especially on the part of men who feel strongly that a male heir must be of the blood line: 'Male hesitancy in adoption is apparently derived from affiliation with groups which uphold traditional kinship values.'[5]—religious groups, for example. Thus the preference for girls really indicates that boys are more highly valued in Western culture, and that adoption is devalued. This makes an amusing contrast with Asian practice, where the high value placed on boys leads them to be the preferred adoptees—indicating that Asian acceptance of adoption as a means of obtaining heirs is much deeper than our own.

All agencies report that nowadays fewer couples request girls, or indeed have any sex preference. This may be a response to the knowledge that waiting lists are longer for girls, but it may also indicate that the sexual egalitarianism of the modern family has gone beyond parental role-sharing and is now affecting the parents' relationships with their children. If egalitarian relationships are the order of the day, a parent will not need a child of the same sex to feel the narcissistic sense of rebirth that is one of the major gratifications of parenthood. The child's behaviour, rather than its symbolic value, will be the source of parental gratification. All this will tend to make adoption psychologically easier for the parents.

Modern parents are also taking steps to ensure that adopted children have experiences as gratifying as those of children who stay with their biological parents. These explorations have gone so far as to involve efforts to breast-feed adopted children—a practice well-known among South African tribal grandmothers, but considered bizarre in the modern world.

One traditional agency social worker described it as 'an attempt to deny the reality of adoption'. But the mothers who are interested in this experiment are often exactly those most open in their acceptance of adoption, and most adventurous in trying to find out what it can mean for the participants. Squeamishness about breast-feeding may even be linked, in a curious way, with squeamishness about adoption—both are aspects of a timid conventionality, if not of neurosis.

LaLeche League International, whose motto is 'Good

mothering through breastfeeding', sees no reason why adoptive parents and babies should be denied the opportunity to become what they describe as 'a thrilled and devoted nursing couple'. They do say that a mother who has never been pregnant might well find the whole business impossible, even if, as they recommend, the baby is placed when it is 1 or 2 days old.

> Nursing an adopted baby is a rather experimental thing in each case ... We are concerned about the possibility that a mother could become so tense and anxious over her attempt to bring in her milk that she would be unable to provide the relaxed, confident mothering that is so important for every baby.

Typical of the new breed of adventurous adopter is one mother who breast-fed the inter-racial, inter-country baby she had adopted after having two of her own:

> I used to squeeze out a few drops of milk every day, just to keep the supply going. I did this for eighteen months, and then I was able to start up again with the new baby. I did want to give him the same start in life as the others.

This is but one example of the many ways in which the commitment of parents has gone further, and for more psychologically healthy reasons, than many adoption professionals were willing to believe possible. It is the parents' groups who have pressed for the adoption of institutionalized children; who have created miracles of family life out of what any social worker would have to regard as unpromising material. Phillida Sawbridge, who runs Britain's Adoption Resource Exchange, has this to say about the limits of adoptability:

> Every time we have set a limit in our minds, it has been challenged and these children have been placed. I did think perhaps it would be children with a limited life expectancy, or severe mental retardation. But now we know that although it may take a lot of time and work, if we really believe that a child can be placed, we will find a family for it.

170

The three kinds of children least likely to be placed, according to a report to 4th N.A.C.A.C., are those with the following sets of problems:

Mentally retarded teenager with physical handicap
Down's Syndrome (Mongolism) retardation
Muscular Dystrophy with limited life span

Social workers are still unsure about what parents can get from adopting children with such very severe problems. Their axiom is that if the parents are not receiving some gratification, they will not be able to go on with the day-to-day struggle of parenting a difficult or unresponsive child.

Some argue that the more unrewarding the task, the better the parent feels about himself for taking it on. The need to be needed may be the strongest motivation of such parents. One social worker put it more sceptically:

Are the parents really equipped to do all this remedial work, taking up their whole adult lives? They're doing it for themselves, out of their tremendous need to have a child. Even the 'room for one more' families—do they have a need to fill their lives, to always have someone around who is dependent on them?

Whatever the motive of adopters, their self-knowledge and confidence seems to be growing, and with it the agencies' trust of them as full partners in the business of finding homes for children in need. Adopters today may have to come to terms with disappointment, disillusion, and frustration, but the strengths they find in themselves as they surmount these things augur well for the success of their families.

9 The Natural Parents

Many of the areas of strain in Western adoption came about because the available children were illegitimate or poor, and the adopters were well-off and respectable. Adoption became a shameful secret, because the child's origins were shameful.

In this century, great efforts have been made to see that the effects of illegitimacy and poverty were not visited upon the child. But as long as the mother was punished, it was inevitable that her child would suffer too. This problem is still unsolved; legislators and taxpayers are still unwilling to 'condone immorality' by giving unmarried mothers adequate support, and the encouragement of adoption can be used as one means of punishing the mother while avoiding the accusation of punishing the child.

It is difficult to draw a psycho-social portrait of the unmarried mother who relinquishes her child for adoption, because she fades from view so quickly after the event. The child is studied, and the adopters are studied, but the aim of the woman who bore the child seems to be to escape study, and in this she has by and large been successful. No one knows what are the permanent effects on her life of this unhappy experience; or whether she relinquished the child because of poverty, youth, inability to cope, or personal ambition. Would she have liked to keep the child, or would she prefer society to stop assuming this to be her wish?

Some answers to these questions can be deduced from the few facts we have. The relinquishment rate varies with the moral and economic climate in different countries. The age and social status of the relinquishing mothers varies too. Beyond this kind of statistical fact, we know little.

Illegitimacy itself is to some extent correlated with low social class, but not nearly to the extent that most people believe. In a 1971 British study, only slightly more than half the mothers were of social class III or below (determined by the father's occupation). The researcher suspected that the relative scarcity of women in classes IV and V stemmed from the fact that these mothers rarely approach social agencies, do not know that there is any alternative to keeping their babies, and thus do not appear in the statistics. The adopters were predominantly from classes I and II.[1]

A Swedish study which includes a survey of the international literature on the subject concludes:

> Few studies have been published that deal specifically with the biological mothers of adopted children. They are usually younger and less well educated than mothers in general, have a poorer economy and housing conditions but otherwise appear to be heterogeneous as regards personality.[2]

Other studies have indicated that it is the youth of the natural mother that induces her to have her child adopted. In 1971 in Britain, over half the relinquishing mothers were under 21. In 1966, 40 per cent of the illegitimate births in the United States were to girls between 13 and 19; this proportion has probably increased.

The National Children's Bureau cohort study in Britain, which followed all the children born in one week of 1958, found that there was no difference in social class between the parents of legitimate and illegitimate children, or between the mothers who kept their babies and those who gave them up. However, there was still a class difference between adopters and relinquishing mothers—this stemmed from the fact that adopters come about half from the middle class and half from the working class, although the population of Great Britain is divided, according to the criteria of the study, into one-third middle and two-thirds working.[3]

This preponderance of middle-class adopters may be the result of agency policies—a theory supported by the fact that more working-class than middle-class adoptions are direct placements, both in Britain and in the United States.

American studies, too, point to the disproportionate number

of middle-class adopters, but they have even less evidence about the natural mothers—except that, these days, many of them are likely to be black. Leontine Young's classic study, *Out of Wedlock*, deals with a group of white unmarried mothers, and is thus not wholly relevant to America today. It was published in 1954, during the high tide of illegitimate white births.

> No one knows how many out-of-wedlock children are born in this country every year. No one knows because the necessity for concealment drives unmarried mothers to subterfuges and deceptions which obfuscate the statistical count.[4]

The book showed that the girls' relationships with their families was disturbed; that one parent or the other was unhealthily dominant in the home; and that the girls usually wanted to present the baby to their mothers—out of revenge, an urge to placate, or a need to repeat their own babyhood. This made the social worker's job easy: all she had to do was to play the role of the girl's mother, and allow the girl to present the baby to her.

Such girls had unusually easy pregnancies, few miscarriages, and a low rate of mortality in childbirth. They were so strongly impelled to their task that it was accomplished with a minimum of difficulty, indeed with a serenity that was very surprising in the circumstances. After the birth, many of the mothers—particularly the ones who chose adoption—felt free to go on with their lives in a more constructive fashion. The emotional conflict had reached its crisis and been resolved.

The pattern revealed in this study is important because it still informs the attitudes of many adopters and adoption workers towards unmarried mothers, even towards those who may conform to quite different patterns.

Whatever their reasons for becoming pregnant, it is clear that American unwed mothers are more likely to give up their babies for adoption than are such mothers in most European countries. Whether this is because of greater mobility and weaker family ties, the influence of fundamentalist religion, or the impossibility of living on the small American welfare stipend, no one is quite sure—all these explanations have been advanced.

174

The desires of adopters are clearly not connected to the rate of relinquishment of babies. Adoption is difficult and not very popular in Eire, for example; but the relinquishment rate is 97 per cent. Adoption is highly popular in Denmark, on the other hand, and in spite of the baby shortage and the queues of waiting adopters, the relinquishment rate is a mere 5 per cent. Public opinion of illegitimacy and social security provisions seem to be the determining factors—not the pressure of frustrated childless couples.

How much support the unmarried mother should receive is a political football in all Western countries. Governor Reagan of California has said that an unmarried mother's third and subsequent illegitimate children should be statutorily removed for adoption. Single parents' organizations think she should receive as much as a foster mother, widow, or anyone else doing the job of raising children on her own.

The National Council for One-Parent Families is an English group that believes economics are at the root of patterns of adoption, relinquishment, and fostering; that inadequate housing and lack of money are responsible for the decisions of many mothers to give up their children.

Mothers in Action is a part of the women's movement that has taken its line from the National Council. Their commentary on the Houghton Report says:

We receive many letters from mothers who have placed their children for adoption or who are about to do so — bitter, unhappy letters. Given better material circumstances, these mothers could have provided loving, happy homes for their children. In Britain, today, the birth and subsequent adoption of their children subjects them to mental and emotional torture from which many never recover.

Claimants' unions, agitating for better court machinery to ensure a deserted mother's maintenance payments; organizations of welfare mothers in the United States; hostels and shelters for young girls who want to keep their babies—these are some of the organizations that stand half-way between the women's movement and the rescue of the unsupported mother.

Adoption is not universally vilified by these groups; but it is seen as something that can and should be made practically unnecessary.

On the other hand, adoptive mothers too have groups that are closely allied to women's liberation. They protest against the discrimination faced by adopters in such matters as maternity benefit and leave, and advocate self-selection by adopters rather than agency screening. These groups often include both parents, and in contrast to the mothers alone (who naturally de-emphasize the male role), the couples are striving for egalitarian marriage.

For women in any branch of the women's movement, motherhood is not necessarily something they want to avoid — it is something they want to do on their own terms. The longing for children produced by involuntary childlessness seems to operate just as strongly with them as with more traditional women — there are few whose reaction is 'Great — now I can get on with the things I really want to do.'

But the women's movement is in a dilemma over adoption. Clearly it must take the side of the impoverished mother alone — material circumstances must not force her to give up her child. Equally clearly, adopters must not be discriminated against — their families should be seen as equal to natural families in every way. Adopters involved in the movement like to see themselves as being on the side of the person who needs them: the child without a family. By the same token, they are most disturbed by the idea that they may be contributing to the oppression of the natural mother. They want to be seen as helpers, not as selfish people gratifying their own wishes.

The figures showing that adopted children do better than those who stay with their unmarried mothers can be used by both sides in the argument. The adopters say it vindicates their role; the unmarried mothers, that it proves they are unfairly treated by society.

Illegitimacy is no longer something that happens invariably by accident or as a response to unconscious needs. It can be a conscious choice. Liberationists are well aware that the only woman who has custody and total legal control over her own children is the unmarried one — although even this ideal situation is being eroded as the courts pay more attention to the

176

rights of the unmarried father. Still, illegitimacy itself does not indicate the necessity for adoption, and as many adoptive parents are finding, when the child asks, 'Why did my mother give me up?' it is inadequate these days to reply, 'Well, you see, she wasn't married …'

The mothers who choose to keep their babies are occasionally the ones who got pregnant deliberately and are well able to cope. But far more often, according to every social worker who deals with them, it is exactly the mothers least able to cope who are most likely to keep their babies. As one explained:

> There are cases where the girl is socially inadequate, has no friends, no relationship with the father—the baby is her only little friend. These are the difficult ones—she has no plans for it but she can't bear to give it up.

Many struggle on for two or three years, but eventually the knowledge that they will never get out of the trap of living on welfare and being alone with the baby—now a demanding toddler—causes the whole situation to break down. The child is now hard-to-place, and everyone would have been better off if he had been adopted soon after birth.

Lynne Reid Banks, whose novel *The L-Shaped Room* was said to be one of the causes of the popularity of unmarried motherhood, has this to say about the impact of her book:

> If I thought my book might have influenced even one girl to keep her baby, and try to bring it up alone, I would hate it. In this third part (of the trilogy), *Two is Lonely*, when my hero says 'the family equation is meant to have two parents', that's me speaking.[5]

Relinquishing a baby for adoption is an index of the pressures in society. The 1958 cohort study, showing how well adopted children are doing at the age of 7, points to a material difference between the adoptive families and others, particularly single-parent families; but where this difference expresses itself most dramatically is in housing. The leading policy implication of the report, some reviewers think, is that special attention should be paid to the housing problems of families with young children.

177

The Mothers in Action report, too, stresses housing as the major practical hurdle to be surmounted by mothers who wish to keep their illegitimate babies. At a time when newly married couples often cannot find a place to live, the threat of eviction from the parental home is often enough to make a girl decide on adoption for her baby.

Society's directives to the unmarried mother are far from clear—in fact, nothing could be more contradictory. If the state pays her a stipend that allows her to keep her child, it is 'condoning immorality'. If she is allowed to relinquish the baby, she is 'getting away with it'. This double bind has not eased in the permissive age: now, if she gives up her baby, she is faced with the example of others who have managed to keep theirs; if she keeps it, social scientists tell her that she is not giving it the best start in life.

Relinquishing the baby, although agencies besieged by adopters are doing their best to make it easy for her, has become more of a problem in recent years. In the days when people still talked about 'getting into trouble' and 'making a mistake', the solution was easy. Painful, but straightforward: mother and baby both deserved the chance of a fresh start.

Today there is no such moral code to rely on. Society finds the relinquishing mother unnatural, and does not pretend to understand her. No one finds understanding more difficult than the adoptive parents, who have waited so long for a child. Their baffled reactions range from 'I thank her every day for being so courageous' to 'I couldn't have done what she did'. One admitted, 'I know there is a girl out there suffering, and I don't like to think about her.'

Ironically, the changes in society that have made it easier to be a single mother have also made it easier to be an adoptive parent. Family life nowadays is often temporary, contingent, and haphazard. The single mother is no different in daily life from that even more common phenomenon, the divorced mother. An adoptive family is in some respects like a step-family. The movement for single-parent adoptions is gaining ground, which should make both ordinary adoptive families and single natural mothers feel positively conventional.

Single mothers these days are still subject to social, economic, and familial pressures that influence their decisions. But it seems

178

that their area of free will is growing. What they would like more than anything else, as researchers find out when they bother to ask, is to make their own decisions. They dislike being manipulated by someone else's policy.

One area in which policy has clashed with mothers' wishes is that of caring for the baby in the days after its birth. Most of the professional workers in hospitals and mother-and-baby homes believe that it is helpful for the mother to care for her baby for a few days, even if she is already firmly committed to adoption. 'Mourning is necessary for mental health', they argue. In England, the mother usually cares for her own child (sometimes even breast-feeding it) for six weeks, until the initial consent to adoption can legally be signed.

Opinion in the United States and Israel, to give two examples, has been preponderantly on the other side. If the mother has decided on adoption, she need not even see the baby, and placement is as early as possible.

Which attitude is the more coercive? One study of English unmarried mothers, not all of whom gave up their babies, showed that:

A very large proportion of mothers (more than four out of five) would have preferred to give their consent only once and to have that final as soon as it was given. Many wanted the baby placed early, preferably directly from the hospital to adoptive parents ... Mothers spoke with great feeling about the lack of choice they had experienced in regard to seeing and caring for the baby in hospital.[6]

More of the girls felt they were being persuaded (mostly by social workers) to keep the baby than felt encouragement to give it up—social workers have so often been accused of exerting pressure in the other direction that they are obviously leaning over backwards. The British consent procedure, too, was designed to give the natural mother a full opportunity to change her mind—which turns out to be the last thing she wants. Typically her views on the desirability of early placement echo those of Anna Freud—who is so often accused of penalizing the natural mother and favouring the adopters.

It has been said that the social work profession is now moving in the direction of treating its clients more like competent human beings. If adoptive parents are to become colleagues in the adoption process, perhaps single mothers can also be seen as adults making conscious decisions, not as themselves infants, swept by forces that can be manipulated by every other party to the transaction.

Ease of relinquishment, however, may yet founder on another obstacle: the wishes of the unmarried father, who until very recently was a complete non-participant. In law as in practice, he has had no rights at all. The unmarried mother could effectively exclude him by refusing to name him, even if he wished to claim paternity. Even where she wished to sue him for child support, the process of getting and enforcing a court order has been so long and tedious that most unmarried mothers have not bothered with it.

In law to this day, the illegitimate child is fatherless. His mother is his legal guardian and custodian, and she alone may consent to his adoption. Two 1972 decisions of the United States Supreme Court have begun to change the situation drastically. Although their implications in various states are not yet clear, and must be established by legal precedent, the cases Stanley vs. Illinois and Rothstein vs. Lutheran Social Service of Wisconsin promise to have far-reaching effects. The United States Department of Health, Education and Welfare warns:

> From these cases, it would appear that a putative father, known or unknown, has rights to the custody of the child, which must be dealt with before the child may be securely placed for adoption. The putative father must be given an opportunity to show his fitness as a custodian. If he is known, he should be personally served in any litigation which would affect his rights. If he is unknown, or if his whereabouts are unknown, service by publication would be necessary.[7]

Why has this consideration suddenly been recognized, after centuries of neglect? Fathers are taking a greater domestic role in all families, and it may be that this reflects not only the wishes of the women, but recognition by men themselves that a close relationship with a child is a desirable part of life.

10 The Adoptees

Adoption works because being a parent is not a matter of blood relationship, but of caring, nurturing, and the day-to-day business of raising a child. This at any rate is the faith of adopters, and they have received support in recent years from the students of animal ethology and human attachment behaviour.

One might expect that biologists would emphasize the biological link in their studies. But whether or not they started out with the idea that the blood tie is all-important, the ethologists have certainly abandoned it by now. The 'imprinting' of young ducks and geese (the mechanism by which the first animate creature they see is treated as their mother) works equally well with adults of their own species or with human scientists, whose books are full of comical accounts of researchers going for walks followed by lines of ducklings. Some of the classic studies of attachment behaviour involve young monkeys and the scientists who have raised them: the outcome of these studies gives clear evidence that whether the attachment is biological or adoptive is not significant.

Not surprisingly, students of human attachment behaviour make no distinction between infants raised by their natural mothers and those adopted before the age of 6 months: it is now thought to be the third quarter of the first year that produces individualized attachment, with consequent mourning if the mother-figure is changed thereafter.

This kind of thinking has immeasurably influenced adoption placement practice, but it leads to some confusion when we attempt to see how adoption works in different societies. The Western theory of attachment has to be modified to explain the working of kinship fostering, or the successes in the adoption of older children that have recently been documented. What in fact is attachment, and how does it work?

Anything the infant does to attract and keep attention, and all his signs of distress when attention is not forthcoming, are signs of his attachment to the adult who takes care of him. Attachment behaviour was thought by Freud to be learned — that is, the infant engages in random activities, and when he finds that crying elicits food, and smiling elicits play, these behaviours are reinforced. Although there is certainly some feedback of this kind, all the attachment behaviour shown in the first year of life is now believed to be instinctive. That is, the infant will engage in it no matter what the response; and moreover, it will appear at the same time in each infant, no matter what his individual experiences.

In a revealing (if rather inhuman) experiment carried out at the University of Virginia in the 1930s, an experimental psychologist and his wife adopted two female non-identical twins of north European stock at 36 days of age, and systematically studied their behavioural development during the ensuing 14 months under conditions of greatly reduced social stimulation.[1]

The infants smiled at the standard time although the 'parents' never smiled at them, and there was no difference in the age at which they manifested all forms of attachment when compared with infants reared normally. Incidentally, one is tempted to wonder whether the researchers would have performed the same experiment on any but adopted children.

The infant follows instinctive patterns of behaviour to elicit certain reactions from his environment. He is ensuring as far as he is able that he will be given the care necessary for survival and protected from predators. This is why Dr Bowlby, the leading theorist of attachment, concludes that it is as instinctually important for species survival as mating and parenting behaviour.

Other scientists, too, have investigated the way a human infant manipulates his environment. Their conclusions are that far from being the helpless thing of conventional description, he is a powerful determinant of the nature of his care and the behaviour of those around him. The fascinating studies of Dr Mary Ainsworth at Johns Hopkins University have shown that an infant whose mother responds fully to his demands during the first year of life cries less, is more independent, and is more obedient to commands than a child whose mother has been more unresponsive or more disciplinarian in her approach. Far from learning not to cry when he finds that it does not produce results, which is the assumption of much child-training theory, if he is satisfied by the response to his cries, he can then stop. Self-centred and demanding behaviour is more likely to be produced by disciplinarian mothers than by responsive ones.

It is our view that infants are genetically biased towards interaction with other people from the beginning ... If an infant is reared in a social environment not too dissimilar from that in which the species evolved — an environment in which adults are responsive to the signals implicit in his behaviour — it seems likely to us that he will gradually acquire an acceptable repertoire of more 'mature' social behaviours without heroic efforts on the part of his parents specifically to train him to adopt the rules, proscriptions, and values that they wish him to absorb.[2]

Instead of parenting being inherent in the adult, it now seems clear that much of it is elicited by the infant. The debate about what touches off maternal behaviour — the pain of childbirth, the hormones, suckling, caring — is rather academic when looked at from this standpoint. Child-care experts from Dr Spock onwards have urged parents to follow their natural inclinations — in other words, to take heed of the dictates of the baby.

It seems logical to ask whether there is not in fact some similar instinctual programming in the adult. But while caring for a baby is necessary to the baby's survival, it is not necessary to the adult's survival. Therefore it is the baby's behaviour that is programmed; the adult's is elicited.

True enough, a new mother learns in two or three days to recognize her own baby's cry, and it becomes difficult for her to relax while it is going on. But this is true of whoever has charge of the infant, whether or not it is the natural mother. Breast-feeding can reinforce such a bond: the mother, too, feels tension as feeding-time approaches, and it is a relief for her as well as for the child. But again, this works for whoever is feeding the child—not only for the woman who has given birth to it.

Attachment, then, happens with the baby's caretaker, whoever it is. But it is even more specific than that: it is a relationship between the child and a specific individual; and as soon as he has learned to recognize that individual, he will suffer distress if his caretaker is changed. It is this characteristic of attachment that the theorists are still unable to define. Broadly, they say that if an infant has experienced one gratifying attachment, it will be easier for him to establish another. Thus he will mourn the loss of the first caretaker, but still be capable of loving the next one. If he has been deprived of the opportunity to make such an attachment at the optimum time (probably between 6 months and 1 year old), it will be more difficult for him later. His relationships with people ever afterwards will be superficial and unsatisfying.

When does the damage produced by change or deprivation become irreversible? Why do some children seem to survive it and others not? How can one measure the quality of such a relationship in order to decide, for example, whether to return the child to his natural mother or leave him in a foster placement?

These are questions to which adoption workers would dearly like to know the answers. It is very difficult to find a way to measure the quality of attachment: so difficult in fact that assessing the effects in later life of these early experiences is almost impossible. One can speculate that a healthy child and a deprived child from the same children's home may have had different experiences while there, in the form of attachment to one or other of the nurses; but how does one find the evidence to support such a speculation?

Most researchers are now convinced that there must be something in it. Bowlby, Ainsworth and others have accumulated a mass of data on maternal deprivation, and described the typical features:

superficial relationships;
no real feeling—no capacity to care for people or to make true friends;

an inaccessibility, exasperating to those trying to help;
no emotional response to situations where it is normal—a
  curious lack of concern;
deceit and evasion, often pointless;
stealing;
lack of concentration at school.[3]

They detail the conditions that produce these responses:

(a) Lack of any opportunity for forming an attachment to
    a mother-figure during the first three years.
(b) Deprivation for a limited period—at least three months
    and probably more than six—during the first three or
    four years.
(c) Changes from one mother-figure to another during the
    same period.[4]

Most of the children studied to produce these results had
suffered more complete deprivation than is likely in any
fostering situation, or in an inadequate home that finally breaks
down. Children in institutions, hospitals, or a series of temporary foster homes regress much faster than children transferred, for example, from a long-term foster home to an adoptive
home. It is very much a question of degree, and one child may
be capable of surviving emotionally in a situation that would
leave another permanently scarred.

In the light of these findings, Anna Freud and her colleagues
have urged that child placement be treated as an emergency
priority, and that such decisions be made with 'all deliberate
speed', and according to the 'child's sense of time'.

While these precepts have found wide agreement, those
attempting to place older children for adoption have not been
deterred by the possibility that the children are already irrever-
sibly damaged. Kadushin's study of children adopted over the
age of 5, after court termination of parental rights because of
neglect or abuse, produced some startling results: 'Adoptions
had been generally as successful as those involving infants with
no history of trauma. This seems surprising, especially considering the history of deprivation which the children had
experienced.'[5]

Kadushin reviewed the literature on long-term outcomes of older-child adoptions, to check his own results. Of a total of 540 children: 'most ... had not been adopted but had remained in long-term foster care. As adults, these children did not differ from any other group.'[6]

What are we to make of these findings? Perhaps it is true, as Christopher Jencks has suggested in *Inequality*, that adult success is a matter of chance as much as anything.

Whatever the disagreements of the professional students of attachment, on a practical level everyone involved in an adoption has noticed its unsettling effects on the child: persistent crying, refusal to sleep or eat, regressive behaviour. Our commonsense reaction tells us that these are dangerous and disturbing experiences. One mother even described her impressions of a pre-adoptive child in a hospital nursery:

> When I was in the hospital having Emily, I was in the nursery feeding her one night, and a new baby came up. But it hadn't been washed or anything, like the others. I asked the nurse what was the matter, and she said, 'Oh, it doesn't have its mother.' The mother was in another part of the hospital, and it had been agreed that she wouldn't see her baby because it was going to be adopted. So they hadn't bothered to clean it up, to make it nice for her to hold. And for the next few days, the nurses fed the baby the way they do, holding it out in front of them, then just putting it back. All the other babies were being cuddled and held, and this baby was just lying there in the nursery the whole time. And I swear that by the time I left, that baby looked different from the other babies, and acted differently.

What does this kind of experience do to a child? How persistent are its effects? The fact is that nobody knows, although they suspect that it has something to do with the behavioural difficulties of adopted children.

Persistent feelings of rejection and alienation have been documented even in the most-loved adopted children, as one unusually dispassionate adoptee wrote:

I am adopted, in my late 20s and married with my own children. I knew of my adoption from the beginning and, although loving my adopted parents, I still felt a great curiosity about my natural parents. This is natural and does not necessarily reflect on the adopted parents ...

I still feel a sense of rejection, regardless of my natural mother's reasons, and she did have ample reasons.

No set of parents could have loved a child more than my adopted parents, yet this sense of rejection persists.

Now that I have my own children, I have reinforced my belief that, except in very rare cases, no one can love a child as its natural parents can.[7]

Adopters might well be tempted to dismiss this vague feeling with 'Well, what can I do about it? We all experience feelings of rejection at some time in our lives—is this really so serious?'

Perhaps not in itself; especially as the woman has met most of the criteria of 'successful outcome' by establishing her own family. But it can provide a clue to one of the most interesting changes in the current adoption scene—the movement of adoptees wanting to know who their natural parents were. This has long been dismissed by adoption professionals: 'If your relationship with your adopted child is a happy and secure one, he will not need or want to search for his first parents. He will know that *you* are his real parents.'

This line has been contradicted by many adoptees, who insist that it is their civil right to have access to information about their origins. But the professionals are right in one sense: those who have actually searched have typically been those unhappy with their adopters, who were told late or ineptly about the fact that they were adopted. In Scotland, the adoption records are open to adult adoptees, and a study has been done of the relatively few who tried to trace their natural parents.

The general picture gained from the majority of adoptees searching for their origins was one of unhappiness and inner pressures and worries making coping with life situations a great effort ... Irrespective of the quality of their home life, the adoptees experienced the surrender by the natural mother as a rejection.[8]

It is mainly adoptive parents who are tempted to believe that this kind of curiosity is unhealthy. People unconnected with adoption generally say, 'I'm sure that if I were adopted, I would want to know.' The proposed Adoption Bill in England would give adoptees the right to search; the Home Office official who keeps track of letters to Members of Parliament on the subject says: 'The letters we get have been reflecting the fears of the adoptive parents that the adolescent child might reject them; the natural mothers haven't been speaking up about this at all.' The overt reasoning of the adopters is that the woman who has started another life without her child will not want him to appear on the doorstep, perhaps to the surprise of her new family. The adoptees retort that this is not what they want either; they would like to see a clearing-house of requests established, or for the agencies to act as go-betweens.

The most famous searcher is an American woman, Florence Fisher, who was never told of her adoption and spent years finding out the truth and tracing her natural parents. She succeeded in the end, and wrote *The Search for Anna Fisher* about her efforts to challenge the bureaucracy of hospitals, lawyers, and relatives that she saw as engaged in a conspiracy of silence against her. She says 'Fear and the unknown are inextricably linked,' and that adoptive children suspect the worst until they know the truth. (In the Scottish study, many of the adoptees suspected that their mothers had been prostitutes, which was in no case the truth.)

The organization founded by Florence Fisher is the Adoptees' Liberty Movement Association, ALMA. This and other groups have increased their membership dramatically in recent years and begun to campaign for 'open adoption': a term which now includes participation by the natural parents in the child's placement and development. They point out that searchers who have found their natural parents never report that it made them more unhappy—at worst, the result has been relief at finally being able to forget about the whole question; at best, it has been genuine joy. If that is so, why not unseal the records?

The irony is that by searching, the adoptees themselves are implicitly denying the validity of adoption and asserting the importance of the blood tie. Why do they feel so strongly—for of the strength and sincerity of their feelings there can be no doubt—that meeting their natural parents will tell them who they are? Are they merely reflecting the mores of Western society as a whole, or does this trend reveal a basic flaw in the practice of adoption? It is likely that the laws will gradually change, that clearing-houses will be established and records at least partially unsealed. Then we will be able to see more clearly what the adoptees actually learn from their searches, and whether their 'genealogical bewilderment' is deepened or dispelled.

Whether or not most adoptees will search for their original parents under the new conditions has yet to be seen. But a recent study makes clear that the desire for more information about their origins is common to most adopted people. A sample of adoptees between the ages of 21 and 30, and their adoptive parents, were interviewed. Both groups asserted that adoption had been a success, and that parents and children were very close in their families. But many more of the adoptees felt that they had psychological limitations or handicaps than were attributed to them by the parents. The parents seemed more committed to seeing adoption in a favourable light, and less willing to admit that there had been any problems. They chose to adopt, and the children did not choose to be adopted; perhaps this is the explanation of these differences in perception.

The most interesting difference between the generations was in the matter of telling. A quarter of the adopters said they had given full and truthful information about the first parents, but only one-tenth of the adoptees believed this to be the case. Moreover:

> more than half the adoptees said they had pressed for additional information about their biological parents but … only one-fifth of the parents interviewed gave the same report … almost three times as many sets of parents as young adults asserted that the adoptees had never voluntarily raised the subject …[9]

It could be, indeed, that the adopters' exaggerated faith in adoption and their unwillingness to countenance what they see as threats to it are sources of strength in the family relationship. Many adoptees have reported that they did not ask further questions about their first parents out of love for their adopters and desire to avoid hurting them. Many see the lies their adoptive parents have told about their origins as loving efforts to protect them. This is an area where rules are hard to establish.

The extra security provided by adopters' insistence on the fact that the child belongs to his new family may more than compensate for the change of caretaker experienced by the adopted child. Bowlby's more recent work indicates that the threat of separation hanging over a child's head for a long time is more damaging and anxiety-producing than a single change of attachment figure followed by security. Mothers alone are likely to consider (and therefore to threaten) giving up the child. In addition: 'the young children of young single-handed mothers are very apt to be subjected to periods of unstable substitute care.'[10]

The definition of foster care has generally been in contrast to that of adoption. The ideal foster parent is not supposed to become too attached to the child, but to be always ready to relinquish it. If attachment does occur, the foster relationship has failed; children have even been moved from their foster homes because the foster mother was becoming too possessive.

It is slowly being recognized that this theory goes against the reality of living with young children; foster parents may soon be given priority in applications for adoption. But there are many problems in giving legal status to fostering with a view to adoption, as a recent English report makes clear:

> The trouble with giving foster parents rights is that many parents would refuse to allow their children to be fostered if they thought there was a risk of losing their child. There are already an estimated 10,000 children being privately fostered, some of them living in appalling conditions, and their numbers would inevitably grow if authorized foster parents had a guarantee to adopt after a number of years.[11]

Thus it is not adopted children as such, but children at risk throughout their early lives who are likely to suffer maternal deprivation and the interruption of attachment. And although the name of Bowlby has been used to attack adoption and to elevate the rights of the natural mother, Bowlby himself says:

confidence in the accessibility and responsiveness of attachment figures, or a lack of it, is built up slowly during all the years of immaturity and ... once developed, expectations tend to persist relatively unchanged throughout the rest of life.[12]

An adopted child has every opportunity to build up these feelings; a child with inadequate natural parents does not. This is more important than the single fact of adoption.

11 Genetics

The role of genetics in adoption has changed appreciably over the years, as the debates about it among the general public have become more sophisticated. Even so, the idea that heredity is a determinant of character, and that 'you don't know what you're getting' when you adopt, has persisted.

The West's fervent belief that intelligence, personality, and all kinds of skills are inherited is not shared by other cultures. The Oriental preference for adopting relatives is not based on these ideas, but rather on the fear that adopting an unrelated person will involve the family in all sorts of transactions with *his* relatives—it is a social preference rather than a personal one.

Adopters may themselves have sorted out their attitude to the genetic lottery by the time they adopt. But it is certainly one of the levers used by relatives, neighbours, the children's teachers, and so on to bring any remaining uncertainty to the surface. To many people, heredity is a blanket explanation of human variety. They say of a child who is good at anything from mathematics to tennis: 'I wonder where he gets that from?' If the grandson of a doctor enrols in medical school: 'Funny how it skips a generation.'

Against this background, it is easy to see how difficult the idea of adoption becomes for many families. Entirely typical is the reaction of one Englishwoman:

> My sister adopted three children, and I have been so interested to see how it worked out. We all thought she was so brave to do it. She believed, you see, that a good up-bringing, the best of everything, an English public school and all that, could overcome their heredity.

But the eldest, the boy, in spite of all she did for him, went and got a girl pregnant. He hadn't changed at all, you see. Well, it just broke my sister's heart. She died a year later.

Then the second child, a girl, got a very rare hereditary sort of brain fever, and died very young. Fortunately my sister wasn't still there to see it.

In any conventional family that includes adopted children, the children's unknown ancestry provides an obvious scapegoat for any and all family misfortunes.

The adoption agencies have traditionally practised 'matching' as an attempt to make it easier for adoptive parents and children to identify with each other. This practice has fallen into disrepute not so much as a result of new ideas about heredity, but because of the impossibility of matching many of today's adoptable children to their prospective parents.

There is no way of knowing whether matching was ever successful, in the sense of making adoption easier for the participants. Every story that ends: 'It's as if she was born to us' can be countered with one that goes: 'I simply don't understand that child.' To complicate the issue, this is a feeling that natural children have too:

The term 'family romance' is applied to a common psycho-analytically disclosed childhood fantasy: the child fancies that his parents are not his real progenitors; his real parents are famous and powerful, and his birth is shrouded in mystery.[1]

Alienation or belonging are obviously determined by more complex issues than whether the child's height or colouring are those of his adoptive parents.

The components of personality are, as we have seen, there to some extent at birth: newborn babies vary enormously in their irritability or placidity and their response to stimuli. But what this means in terms of later behaviour is anything but clear, just as it is still unclear how much the genetic component of intelligence affects later performance.

The new debate about genetics is composed of a muddle of

several issues. Intelligence, particularly alleged racial differences in I.Q., has had most of the headlines. But perhaps more important to adopters is the debate about what is known as the cycle of deprivation. Is it true that the poor have only themselves to blame, in the sense that inability to make a living and raise children adequately are related to low intelligence, and that children of these families, because of their genetic inheritance, will repeat the performance no matter what their early life experiences?

Parents with low intelligence provide a less stimulating environment for their children than those with high intelligence. Thus the children of such families are likely to have both heredity and environment working against them. This is one reason why it is so difficult to sort out the effects of each.

There is, however, a good deal of evidence that adopters need not worry about the ability of a stimulating environment to break through this pattern. The evidence may be incomplete, but what there is of it mostly confirms the benefits afforded by a healthy environment.

The workings of the vicious circle are well described by Bowlby.

> Because ... children tend unwittingly to identify with parents and therefore to adopt, when they become parents, the same patterns of behaviour towards children that they themselves have experienced during their own childhood, patterns of interaction are transmitted, more or less faithfully, from one generation to another. Thus the inheritance of mental health and of mental ill health through the medium of family microculture is certainly no less important, and may well be far more important, than is their inheritance through the medium of genes.[2]

It is now well known that the I.Q. of children in institutions gets progressively lower—an effect that is reversed by adoptive placement. This kind of result seems to invalidate much of the heredity argument, as well as raising the question of whether whatever it is that I.Q. tests measure can possibly be as innate and immutable as the testers have claimed.

Harold Skeels has done some of the most famous experiments

194

in this area, using adopted children as one means of determining the relative effects of heredity and environment. His on-going study of children placed from an institution, compared with a group that stayed there, showed that as adults, all the adopted children were self-supporting, while the others had suffered progressive mental retardation.

Most important for our purposes is a final study of a group of adopted children he has been following since 1949. His conclusions are worth quoting because this is a study that has been used as ammunition by both sides in the debate.

Preliminary indications are that these adoptive children as adults are achieving at levels consistently higher than would have been predicted from the intellectual, educational, or socio-economic level of the biological parents, and equal to the expectancy for children living in the homes of natural parents capable of providing environmental impacts similar to those which have been provided by the adoptive parents.[3]

Does this mean that the children are achieving as if they were born to their adopters? At least it seems to say that the effects of environment outweigh, if not totally eliminate, those of heredity. Skeels concludes:

it would seem that we have adequate knowledge for designing programs of intervention to counteract the devastating effects of poverty, socio-cultural deprivation, maternal deprivation, or a combination of these ills.[4]

All our experts would agree with him so far. Children who grow up in children's homes end up in other institutions — prisons and mental hospitals. Children in depriving environments re-create these environments in their turn. Adopted children become perfectly normal members of society.

Policy-makers and social workers are concerned about how these findings can be implemented. At what stage is the state justified in intervening, and replacing a depriving natural family with a healthy adoptive one?

Adopters are concerned about something else again. If they interest themselves in this debate at all, they are likely to ask

whether their children will disappoint them in terms of intelligence and achievement—and this worry is not confined to
adopted children. They tend to take comfort from the environ-
mentalists, and to be on their side of the argument. A London
social worker says they are right to do so:

> People are so irrational about heredity. 'The mother must
> be a nurse or a student'—they never think about the father.
> Or they think heredity correlates with occupation. One
> professional man wanted kids of intelligent parents, but he
> ended up with a son with 90 IQ. That boy is now in medi-
> cal school. When I compare him with our kids in care who
> have 90 IQ!

One of the leading I.Q.-debaters, Dr Eysenck, has pointed
out that because of 'regression to the mean', highly intelligent
parents are likely to have children less intelligent than themselves. If adopters, as we know, are above average in intelligence
and achievement, this would apply to them whether they
adopted or bore their children—both kinds would be a cross-
section of abilities.

Many social scientists have tried to opt out of the whole
controversy, and to point out its trivial nature. Christopher
Jencks and his collaborators have said:

> Economic success seems to depend on varieties of luck and
> on-the-job competence that are only moderately related to
> family background, schooling, or scores on standardized
> tests. The definition of competence varies greatly from one
> job to another, but it seems in most cases to depend more
> on personality than on technical skills.[5]

Is economic success the criterion by which most parents would
evaluate their children? Competence at a job may not be
related to other areas of competence such as family life.

But this kind of evaluation has been at the root of the most
highly politicized part of the whole argument—the debate over
the I.Q. differences between American blacks and whites. The
opening salvo came from an article by Arthur Jensen, who
claimed:

The basic data are well known: on the average, Negroes test about 1 standard deviation (15 IQ points) below the average of the white population in IQ ... When gross socio-economic level is controlled, the average difference reduces to about 11 IQ points ... which, it should be recalled, is about the same spread as the average difference between siblings in the same family.[6]

Subsequent researchers have found that black children perform differently on I.Q. tests depending on whether the tester is black or white; that Jensen has not used all the possible controls on 'gross socioeconomic level', and that strict controlling for these factors erased the whole 15-point difference. Others postulate that nothing can erase the feeling of inferiority induced by racism—would a black person who had just read the Jensen article be likely to do well on an I.Q. test?

These considerations make the whole issue seem slightly ludicrous, but it is very much part of the inter-racial adoption controversy. Blacks claim that it is another example of whites hiding their racism under the cloak of objectivity, and a further reason why no white family should be allowed to adopt a black child. Do white inter-racial adopters worry about it at all? Some of the issues were sorted out by an adoption worker with a great deal of experience in trans-racial placement.

I think the parents are worried about Jensen but won't say so. Most inter-racial adoptions are of mixed-race children anyway, so it doesn't really apply. The ones who adopt all black kids are either liberal intellectuals who don't believe in heredity, or religious people who say we're all God's children anyway.

Jensen and Eysenck are interested in adoption because it can prove or disprove their arguments. But adopters, scornful of the fatalism of the hereditarians, are not very interested in them. In any case, the evidence from adoption studies is by no means clear—both sides cite the same studies in their own support. Jencks is dismissive of the race-I.Q. question: 'Some whites apparently feel that if the average white is slightly more adept at certain kinds of abstract reasoning than the average black, this legitimizes the whole structure of white supremacy—not just in America, but around the world.'[7]

One interesting aspect of the difference in learning behaviour between whites and blacks postulated by Jensen is that although he saw black schoolchildren as slower at gaining cognitive skills, he described them as more socially adept than the white children. Dr Kellmer Pringle noticed the same thing among deprived English children: 'there is evidence to suggest that where environmental demands for social independence are very pressing, there is a tendency for children to become rather precocious socially.'[8] A genetic hypothesis seems unnecessary here.

Other areas of competence besides intelligence can, of course, also be affected by the inherited qualities Jensen talks about. Components of personality and mental health are, according to Jencks, even more closely related to job success. But here, too, we are quickly faced with the supremacy of the environment.

R. D. Laing has shown how family interaction can produce or exacerbate mental illness in one member of the family—often a kind of scapegoat. Bettelheim, too, emphasizes the role of the social environment in producing personality changes—an emphasis that helps to explain the dramatic successes in the adoption of deprived children: 'Psychoanalysis is by no means the most effective way to *change* personality. Being placed in a particular type of environment can produce much more radical changes, and in a much shorter time.'[9]

Jencks's final recommendation is that to eliminate inequality, we should simply eliminate it—political measures should be taken to equalize incomes, rather than hoping vainly that intervention in the school system will do the job for us. He would say that Skeels is right—we do know enough to counteract the effects of deprivation. In a society that refuses to take such drastic but effective measures, adoption will be part of the patching-up process that tries, after the fact, to make up for the effects of inequality. It is effective for the children; there is nothing it can do about the lives of their parents.

The debate about inequality has been carried out much more vigorously in the United States than in England, and we can see some reasons for this when we see how the grounds of the debate have shifted. In England it still centres round the 'bad blood' question—many adopters and agencies are not so concerned about the effects of environment, since they believe them to be negligible. They are more preoccupied with matching, to make sure that a 'good' family does not get a child with 'bad' heredity.

The Americans are, by and large, now convinced that environmental intervention, especially of the all-embracing kind offered by adoption, is the major determinant of personality and of competence, both scholastic and occupational. This is one reason why adoption is more widely practised in America than in any other country—it is part of the same massive act of faith that created the Head Start pre-school enrichment programme and is now pressing for admission of more blacks and women to universities and top jobs.

Adopters point out that the effects of inherited characteristics on intelligence are at present almost impossible to sort out. Pre-natal malnutrition and stress during pregnancy are examples of other determinants of a child's I.Q. that may be associated with illegitimacy, and hence with the intelligence of adopted children. Adopters these days are much more likely to mention such factors than to attribute their child's intellectual performance to his genes. The genetic hypothesis was only used by adopters who did not really believe that adoption works; today's adopters, who put their faith in the environment, are logically cut off from such a recourse.

12 The Go-betweens

Adoption agencies have been in existence for almost a century. Today there are close to a hundred of them in Britain alone, and 70 per cent of non-relative adoptions are done through agencies. Legislation is being proposed to ban third-party placements and ensure that all adoptions go through the agencies; two of the United States already have such laws.

The agencies have been a success, then, and have managed to impose most of their ideas about adoption on the general public and the legislators. But at the same time they are the focus of impassioned criticism from many of the groups they serve. Arrogance, irrationality, conservatism, prejudice—these are some of the charges levelled against agencies by their clients.

In the nature of things, the agencies now must disappoint many more potential adopters than they can gratify. For everyone who says, 'They were so understanding, and found us the perfect baby', there are ten or more who have been turned down—and whose comments are likely to be 'They're a prying lot of busybodies', or 'They're standing between the children and the people who want to adopt them'.

Such criticism is inevitable, but many agencies try to head it off by holding meetings for disappointed adopters, by explaining to them that the baby shortage is not the agency's doing. Some try to convince such clients that adoption is really not for them, or to induce them to convince themselves. But such tactics often backfire—they convince the disappointed clients of the agency's arrogance and insensitivity.

Another reason why agencies have been the target of criticism is that they are staffed by social workers, whose unpopularity is attested by many sources:

As presidential assistant John Ehrlichman said in an interview in the Wall Street Journal of October 18, 1972, 'I think a President with a substantial mandate, who feels the majority of the people are behind him, will feel very comfortable in saying to a vested interest group, such as the social workers, "Look, your social program of the 1960s isn't working and we're going to dismantle it, so you'll just have to go out and find honest labor somewhere else."'[1]

Social workers may have survived the Nixon Administration (although the amount of public money spent on their activities was severely curtailed), but they have not survived the kind of thinking behind that statement: the idea that practical results, in terms of cost-effectiveness, must be expected almost instantly from any social programme. Related to this is the idea that paying social workers to solve problems of poverty is inappropriate; the money is better spent being given, in some form or other, to the clients themselves.

The first attack comes from the political right; the second usually comes from the left. Between the two, social workers have few defenders. They are the heirs of the resentment felt against the charitable 'lady bountiful' whom they have largely replaced; and there is the inescapable suspicion that they are really the agents of the state, whose aim is to save as much money as possible. It is hard for someone whose stipend has just been cut on the recommendation of a 'welfare snooper' to believe in the goodwill of the next social worker who comes around.

The difference in class origin between social workers and most of the people they serve is another source of strain. Jane Rowe of the A.B.A.A. remarks in her guide to adoption casework, 'Caseworkers are generally very capable people and clients frequently just the opposite.' This at any rate is what caseworkers often seem to make their clients feel.

Commitment of an unusual kind is now being asked of the community-based social worker. Minority groups are demanding that she be from the group she is serving, not a middle-class dilettante.

The contrast in styles they are talking about is summed up by two Washington agencies. In the first, about ten children had been placed for adoption in the past year. Private and prestigious, it does not handle long-term foster care cases, and thus only accepts babies who are likely to be placed immediately. This limits its usefulness to the black community around it. The atmosphere in the building is almost that of a group therapy session, with well-dressed volunteers 'exploring their perceptions' in case-conferences before leaving early to join the car pool.

The next agency is part of the city's social services department, high up in an anonymous concrete government block. The head of adoptions, like all her staff, is black (so is 90 per cent of the city of Washington). As she describes her techniques for finding black adopters, the surrounding neighbourhoods come vividly to life:

> You know, if you go to Woolworth's, there are lounges in the back—we call them the old ladies' clubs. You make sure your phone number is posted there, and that there's always someone on the other end of it. And forget about community leaders. People are always saying find the preacher, or the N.A.A.C.P. man, somebody like that. They're already too far out of touch. What I want is the nosiest lady on the block, whose kitchen is always full of people sitting around.

The contrast was summed up by Alfred Herbert, whose Black Child Development Institute has been helping to set up agencies to reach black adopters.

> The white college girls who go into social work might spend six months in a particular agency, then when they have learned what they can from the situation, they move on, maybe right in the middle of a lot of long-term cases that really need one person to see them through. They really don't have much understanding of the people they're trying to help, and even more important, they don't have the commitment.

Not everyone would agree with him: Spence-Chapin, for

example, makes good use of temporary, often white, trainees. But dealing with underprivileged clients is not the agencies' only problem when it comes to adoption. They have also to deal with over-privileged adopters.

David Kirk has identified one of these areas of stress. The kind of person likely to apply to an adoption agency, he points out, is likely to place a high value on individualism, self-reliance, and independence. He has learned to discipline himself and to expect respect from other people. It goes against the grain to find that he is being judged by someone else, that important decisions affecting his personal life are being made by someone he did not choose. He deeply resents the social worker's role, and the resentment is compounded by the fact that he must dissimulate it to have any chance of success.

The social worker, in turn, may have problems in dealing with him. She is used to feeling superior to her clients, and to disguising this feeling while deriving satisfaction from it. The very competence and self-confidence of the middle-class appli-cant is likely to make her resent him, and to feel that he is trying to take over and make her decisions for her. She strikes back with a response like 'I feel you are not able to relate positively to the agency', or 'You seem to have an intellectual approach to adoption'.

How expert in fact are the social workers, and how much of their expertise is—as some of their clients would charge—simply prejudice dressed up as fact? There are innumerable stories about the narrowness of some of their judgments, but most of the stories indicate that, like the law, social work practice simply codifies the prejudices of the community.

One adopter, interested in agency practice as a civil rights question, said:

The agencies can turn people down without giving any reason, but I found out about two cases that seemed to me extraordinary. One was a man who had been in prison, and didn't tell them because he naturally thought it would ruin his chances. Of course they found out from the official records, and rejected him because he hadn't told them. The other was a communist couple—they said the child would grow up in too bigoted an atmosphere, too different from the rest of society. But they don't say that about Catholics or Plymouth Brethren.

Social workers are often quite explicit about their prejudices. The director of one of London's largest agencies said:

> I would see a red light in the case of the intellectual who sees inter-racial adoption as a flag—the militant atheist. Someday their poor little boy is going to want nothing but a bowler hat and a dark suit, and he isn't going to be allowed to have them!

For every social worker story of this kind, there are many more on the other side. One may reject a couple (as recently happened in London) because the wife earns the money while the husband keeps house; but in the same week, another London worker said: 'I got my committee to approve a family who believe in sexual freedom in marriage!'

Social workers are taking on jobs that are unrewarding, exhausting, and underpaid. Society often blames them for not solving problems that they have not been given the resources to solve. Why didn't the social worker *know* that a baby in her jurisdiction was going to be battered? Why do her foster care placements sometimes break down? Compared with the vast problems she faces every day, the chagrin of a rejected adopter can come to seem trivial.

Social workers have had to surround themselves with a rigmarole of expertise in order to gain the confidence of the people they work with. In a society that prizes university degrees and professional qualifications and delights in being blinded by science, this was a necessary survival tactic. The extra pomposity noticeable in the writings of social workers derives from their status as the step-children of sociology and psychology, from their need to think of themselves as constituting a profession and a discipline.

The social work profession grew up in the post-war years, and its philosophy was heavily influenced by the popular Freudianism of the period. The involvement of social workers in adoption was a response to a specific need: white out-of-wedlock births in the United States jumped from 42,800 in 1943 to 82,500 in 1960.

As D. D. Wachtel reflected in her study of adoption agencies and the adoption of black children: 'one is tempted to speculate that the creation of adoption agencies has been a response to the absolute increase in the number of out of wedlock births to white women.'[2] The social workers in the study were 97 per cent female and 86 per cent white. Because of the nature of their original clientele, they had been trained to believe that an unmarried mother was acting out the last stages in a drama that began with her feelings about her own mother. Leontine Young suggested that because illegitimate pregnancy was so heavily stigmatized, it was chosen by neurotic girls as a means of getting back at their parents. She acknowledged that in societies where it was no disgrace, the unconscious needs of such girls would be likely to find another outlet.

This kind of pop Freudianism was also applied to adopters. Much of the feeling against social workers stems from the era when these ideas were current, but social workers themselves have moved on.

> The presumption was pathology. This is when we were living through the Freudian era in professional goals and we literally approached all clients as pathological. Adoptive parents are remarkably healthy both mentally and physically. They are intelligent people and we should be working with them on a complete give and take basis.[3]

The comedy of the situation is well illustrated by another description of the shift in professional ideas.

> 'Fifteen years ago, if somebody had come to us saying they wanted to adopt a child of another race, we would have thought they were neurotic,' Mr Walter A. Heath, Director of Los Angeles County Department of Adoptions, said recently. 'But now we are committed to the idea that *every* child deserves a home.'[4]

The inappropriateness of the Freudian model became obvious when social workers began trying to serve other groups of clients. The large numbers of babies left in the Philadelphia city hospital by their mothers were evidence of a social and economic problem, rather than a psychiatric one. The break-down rate in black families, the shift in the white population from adoption to abortion—these trends could not be wholly explained by unconscious drives. As a conversation with one black social worker revealed:

> I went to a lecture by a psychologist, who kept saying, 'When you get an unmarried mother, what is the crisis in her life that caused this? Look for the crisis.' Well, I have people whose whole lives are a crisis, so what are you talking about?

The professional orientation of social workers has sometimes stood in the way of their service to clients. They were unwilling to allow adopters to take the risks of adopting 'hard-to-place' children, even when the adopters requested them. Studying the child was occasionally a higher priority than early placement. In the early days of complex adoption, as Bradley found:

> the 'better' couple (was) seen as suitable for the 'better' child and the marginal couple seen as more suitable for the marginal child. At first blush this seemed to raise an ethical question. It also contradicted some of the practice literature with its stress on the need for the 'better' family to handle the problems that might arise with a marginal child.[5]

She concluded that social workers identified with their 'better' couples, and wanted very much to find children good enough for them.

The agencies have been most heavily criticized for their manipulation of supply and demand. Most will admit now that many of their criteria for adopters were only used to weed out excessive numbers, not because they were known to have any-thing to do with adoption outcome. Some agencies now deny that they ever turned down a child, but the record is there—it was one of the commonest means used of controlling the work-load. Wachtel traces the history of this technique:

until recently adoption agencies were being offered more children for relinquishment than they had staff to find adoptive homes for. The agencies generally solved this problem by refusing to accept relinquishment of many of the black children offered them. When abortion became more generally available, many white women chose abortion over adoption for their unwanted children, with the result that adoption agencies were taking many fewer white children into custody. Black women probably began getting abortions too, but the unmet need for adoption had been so great in the past that even with the increase in abortion, there were considerable numbers of black women who desired adoption for their unwanted children. Since adoption agencies now had more free staff time, they were more willing to accept relinquishment of black children, and consequently relinquishment and adoptive placement of black children both increased at the same time that abortion became more available.[6]

The crowning criticism of the social workers was that they did not believe in adoption at all. Any deviation from the norm was seen by the pop-Freudians as fraught with psychological danger, and this attitude extended to adoption. A textbook called *Child Placement Through Clinically Oriented Casework* almost negates its own utility:

The separation of child from parent is perhaps the most tragic occurrence in a child's life. Its unfavorable after-effects are usually irreversible despite the sometimes successful experience of being reared by substitute parents.[7]

Even when they did believe in adoption, they definitely thought it was second-best.

the motive for adopting, if not based upon an organic sterility that precludes having one's own children, might be a neurotic one ... Social workers know that a potentially good mother makes every effort to have her own child before she tries to adopt one.[8]

The clash between the ego of the adopter and the ego of the social worker has proved to be one of the least soluble problems faced by the agencies. Even where social workers see themselves as performing a helping rather than a judging role, they are liable to be hurt by rejection. Their major job satisfaction comes not from money or prestige, but from feeling useful. Not surprisingly, they are wounded by the parents' denial of their usefulness.

After a group meeting for a number of pre-adoptive couples, one worker

> was shocked to learn that, having performed a helping role—which was to elicit pertinent questions, encourage honest answers, engage in role playing, and foster group interaction to draw out individual members—the couples saw the help as coming only from the group.[9]

Another social worker found that the adopters no longer wanted to communicate with her once she had placed a child with them.

> The caseworkers felt effectively shut out by couples who had participated actively during the home study and pre-placement period. For the adopting parents, once they had the baby, the focus seemed to narrow to include only themselves and the child. In talking with the caseworker, they tended to gloss over their problems and to make only platitudinous observations such as 'It is as though he had been with us always.'[10]

This is not the only barrier between social workers and clients. Agency requirements have until very recently included restrictions that both adopters and caseworkers saw as restricting, such as religion. This was a legacy of the Church-based origins of many adoption agencies, and was adhered to tenaciously even when church attendance fell—to less than 5 per cent in England, for example.

Researchers have discovered that some of the unhappiest adoptions are likely to be those by authoritarian parents with strict moral views, and that these attributes are highly correlated with the practice of religion, especially the fundamentalist Protestant varieties. Few agencies allow Christian Scientists to adopt, and some have been known to refuse applications from Jehovah's Witnesses and other sects that cut their children off from the normal life of their society, but adopters of other religious persuasions still have an advantage over confessed unbelievers.

The waning of religion as a prerequisite for adoption has not come about for these reasons, however. It is now seen as an anomaly that the relinquishing mother can choose the religion of her child, when she retains no control over its future in other ways. The state laws requiring that adoptive parents must practise a religion have been challenged in the United States on constitutional grounds of separation of Church and state. In England, the diocesan agencies have turned over much of their responsibility for adoption to the local authorities.

When adoption work is finally taken over by the state, the current argument goes, religious requirements and other bigotries of the private agencies will be ended. There will be no obstacle to the abolition of third-party placements, because everyone will be satisfactorily served by the agencies.

There are many things the social-work tradition of the agencies has to give to children and their adopters. Social workers are working more and more closely with the adoptive parents' groups—using them to recruit new adopters and to disseminate information. They are heeding the advice of Ursula Gallagher, the 'adoption lady' at the United States Children's Bureau, who says: 'Embrace them! Inform them! When they believe that you are really trying to place the children, they can help you. They are the best help you can have in finding new parents.'

The agencies can only gain the confidence of their clients if there is broad agreement in society at large about the aims of their work.

This kind of agreement is beginning to be reached. But there is another powerful force at work on the agencies' side—the desire of legislators and adoptive parents to stamp out the so-called 'grey market' in babies. This is perhaps the main motive behind the laws banning independent placement. The agencies may not be perfect, but they are likely to be better than the alternatives.

On the grey market in New York a baby now costs some-where between $3,000 and $25,000, according to a recent *New York Times* report. There are several lawyers in New York and Miami who specialize in private adoptions, and their fees are rising astronomically as they try to outbid each other for the few babies available. Joseph Spencer of Fifth Avenue, who the *New York Times* calls 'the dean of private adoption', says:

> Money talks in this business. It's gotten to the point where babies that are supposed to go to my clients are being snatched right out from under our noses for more money. There's a terrific hunger out there, and the people who will suffer are those in the $15,000–$16,000 salary bracket or less, because they'll never be able to afford to adopt — unless they have wealthy parents.[11]

One couple, rejected by an agency for being too old (early 40s), received a telephone call from another lawyer:

> If you like, I will mail you photographs of some handsome single young men and beautiful single young women. For $10,000, you can choose the couple you want to make the baby for you.[12]

London's *News of the World* conducted a similar investigation of couples who 'jump the heartache queue', centred around a few doctors in the Harley Street area. Foreign girls having their babies in private nursing homes were one major source for these doctors, and the bribe for inducing a 'respectable' girl to bear a baby for adoption was quoted at £10,000.

From the mass of innuendo in this series, a few interesting stories emerged. One eminent gynaecologist said: 'I know the adoption law backwards, and I won't obey it.' Her object was to avoid the six-week wait before placement that most adoption societies demand; she placed babies directly from her house after three days.

The mothers benefit from grey-market adoption because their private medical expenses are paid and they may even end up with some cash in hand. No agency can compete with the attraction of independent placement on this level.

Adopters often prefer it, too, because the waiting list, the investigation, indeed, all the things they dislike about going through the agency procedure, are avoided. Many feel that they are in control when they adopt privately—that it is *their* decision, as having a baby the usual way would have been.

Although the shortage of babies is currently increasing grey-market activity, the doctors and lawyers who engage in it know that they are likely to be put out of business by legal changes. The tendency for money to become ever more important in adoption is being counteracted by the movement to abolish fees, to subsidize, in fact to make money irrelevant to the choice of parents. For a while, the gap will widen between the rich who turn to the increasingly expensive grey market, and the rest, who turn to the newly accessible agencies for the child who is less easy to place. Then, new laws will ban the middleman, and rich couples will have to find other ways through the system.

One way that the affluent middle class has chosen is overseas adoption. One of the members of Friends of Children of Vietnam told the *New York Times*:

'In the United States, there are three- to five-year waiting lists.' Foreign adoption, she said, seemed the quickest way—despite all the obstacles—'and the need seemed most in Vietnam.' Virtually the only other countries that allow such adoptions are South Korea and some South American countries, the women said.[13]

More than half the requests received by the group are for healthy infant girls, and few of the families who apply are willing to adopt handicapped children. Clearly, international adoption is seen by many as an alternative to the grey market at home as a way of getting the babies who are now unavailable through agencies.

Why, then, attack the practice of third-party placements, when it is an easy and fuss-free way of adopting for so many? The disproportionately large sums demanded may in fact seem an advantage to the natural mother, who not only profits herself from the transaction, but is sure that her baby is going to an affluent family.

Jane Rowe says it is 'to stop the tiny minority of very bad

placements'. Dr Owen says it is 'not aimed so much against the mother who wants to choose her baby's adopters, as against the middleman who is making money out of it'.

Perhaps all the agencies can give is the illusion of fairness, for what makes one person able to adopt a child and another forced to give it up is so manifestly unfair.

13 Conclusion: The Baby Famine

The aim of this study has been to trace the influence of attitudes on practice and of practice on law. We have seen that patterns of adoption interact with patterns in other areas of life—with a society's economy, its system of landholding, and the degree of its industrialization. It is tempting to say, in the end, that if adoption is dependent on these more basic elements, it cannot be changed unless and until they are changed.

It is tempting to say this, but it is also an evasion. Even a determinist is rarely willing to believe that all conscious human effort is futile; certainly everyone who works with children quickly comes to believe that there is no area of human life in which effort is more richly repaid, or more necessary.

What sort of effort, then, should be made to improve our adoption practice? The answer is frequently unclear even to the experts; and movements that seem to hinder adoption actually turn out to help it. Abortion legislation, for example, stems from the belief that no woman should have to raise children she does not want; this philosophy also encourages unwilling mothers to relinquish their children for adoption. Abortion diminishes the baby supply; but as we have seen, this has done more than anything else to help the children actually waiting for adoption. It is unsophisticated to argue, in the words of a new American bumper sticker, ADOPTION—NOT ABORTION.

Changes in the adoption law itself must be similarly scrutinized for their long-term effects. To ban non-agency adoptions, for example, may seem to discriminate against the poor and those who practise informal adoption. But by funnelling everyone through the same system, it may help to ensure that the system operates responsibly and fairly—if the well-off and articulate must use it like everyone else, they will not allow it to deteriorate. The argument for comprehensive state schooling in Britain, with no opting-out for rich parents, follows similar lines.

This is the way political decisions of a very broad and general kind affect individual lives. It is possible to argue, indeed, that certain political systems are inherently incapable of serving the needs of all their members. This is what the socialist countries claim, when they point out that their child-care problems, like their population problems, are well on the way to solution. The capitalist countries of the West reply that only the growth induced by giving free rein to ambition will produce enough wealth to finance a welfare state while preserving political liberty.

The widest political gulf these days, however, does not seem to be that between capitalism and socialism. Indeed, similar effects of falling birth-rate, subsidized adoption, and pressure for early placement and more comprehensive adoption services are currently being observed under both systems. To be sure, if the Western economies deteriorate rapidly in the next few years, the children of the poor will again be risking institutionalization and neglect; but it does seem that any country with a vigorous economy is likely to continue to take its child-care responsibilities more seriously than in the past. The real gulf is between economically strong countries and those with such severe food and population problems that the traditional social structure is disintegrating and not being replaced by anything else. This again calls capitalism into question—is it true that the exporting of underdevelopment has caused many of these problems?

Even in the developed countries, it has recently been argued that no government will continue to finance a welfare state unless it has some control over the numbers it will be supporting —that if it is to continue to provide family allowances, free education, and support for unmarried mothers, it will not allow the indigent to have an unlimited number of children. As yet, this argument has only facetious (Gore Vidal) or fanatical (Governor Reagan) adherents, but if it does capture the attention of political moderates, then accusations of sinister planning under socialism will seem hollow.

The really insoluble problem in Western adoption today is that of supply and demand. Where adopters are well-served, in the sense that they can choose the child of their dreams and adopt it without too much fuss, there is sure to be a large supply of unwanted children, most of whom will never be adopted. Where the children are well-served, with a large enough supply of possible parents so that the right ones can be selected for each child, there are bound to be many disappointed would-be adopters. How can these numbers be manipulated without causing distress on one side or the other?

Convincing people that adoption is not really what they want does not seem to work. The childless are not comforted by the knowledge that many of their friends are consciously deciding against parenthood; and institutionalized children long for parents, no matter how much their peers may want to escape their own families. Accepting one of the alternatives to adoption, however, is often suggested as one means of regulating supply and demand. At present, foster parents are in great demand even though adoptable children are few. People who are primarily interested in the children's welfare, the argument goes, will fit themselves into the system wherever they are needed. Dr Winnicott described his own change of attitude in the late 1950s:

Is it a sign of greater maturity in a married couple when they prefer to adopt or when they prefer to foster? Up to ten years ago, I should have said it was a sign of maturity to prefer to adopt; but now the answer is not so clear.[1]

Even if the supply of unwanted babies dries up completely, and the social services become so competent that relinquishment of older children diminishes, there are some indications that society is beginning to demand higher standards of parenting — and such demands may, in the short term, make more children available for adoption.

The number of battered-baby cases reported continues to double every year, and this may be a sign that parents who wish to relinquish their children still cannot bring themselves to do so. Relinquishment is still not entirely acceptable in our society; but the incidence of child abuse is as sure an indication

215

as the declining birth-rate that the stresses of parenthood are being more keenly felt.

One United States estimate identifies battering as the commonest cause of death in children under 5 years of age. In England, two battered children die every day.[2] And the number of children suffering unreported physical abuse is incalculable. Doctors are beginning to be more suspicious, and to pay more attention to the possibility of battering when they treat injuries to children; but there is still great reluctance on the part of social workers and health visitors to report suspected cases and so lose the trust of the parents.

Dr Kellmer Pringle suggests that the attitude to children today is what the attitude to women was fifty years ago: they are chattels. And just as divorce has become the normal solution to marital strain, legal separation between hostile parents and children will surely be increasingly possible. The very existence of adoption laws is one step in this direction: they were the first challenge to the inalienability of parental status. Revocable adoption, on the analogy of divorce, is part of the most modern adoption laws. It is time that biological parenthood became revocable too.

Even such sophisticated methods, however, will affect only a few children—never enough to satisfy the demand for adoptable babies. More fanciful solutions to the baby famine have recently been suggested. The American answer is, predictably, that private enterprise should fill the breach. The catalogue that one New York lawyer sent to his childless clients, enabling them to choose the parents of their baby for $10,000, is one such scenario. Like so many aspects of the American social system, this has one obvious disadvantage: only the rich can afford it. A very different answer has been suggested in England, by a general practitioner writing in a medical journal:

That society is instinctively generous is witnessed today by the Blood Transfusion Service. Why should there not be a parallel Baby Donor Service where those couples who are fortunate to be fertile would donate their third and subsequent babies to Adoption Societies? ... Child-bearing is infinitely safer than in previous years. Some couples are natural child-producers ... Adequate financial compensation should be provided by the Government for such public-spirited parents.[3]

This is the suggestion one might expect to emerge from welfare-state, National Health Britain. The analogy with blood donation is striking: Richard Titmuss's classic study of the subject, *The Gift Relationship*, gave a comparison between British and American practice. He concluded that where the service was voluntary, unpaid, and free to the user, it worked better in all ways (number of willing donors, quality of the blood donated, availability when needed) than where it was a free-market operation. Paid donors in the United States had a high incidence of hepatitis and other disqualifying diseases, and the blood was stockpiled to wait for high prices. He concluded that the instinctive generosity of society should be tapped—and that the more this was done, the more society was strengthened and the better its citizens felt about their role in it.

Applying the same principle to babies creates some problems —giving a pint of blood is an infinitely less serious operation than spending nine months on the gestation of a child. What is 'adequate financial compensation'? How can it be fixed to encourage people without spoiling the 'gift relationship', or creating a population boom?

It is the population question that, in the last analysis, makes all such suggestions improbable. If adoptable babies were readily available, what sort of demand for them would there be? If it were ten times the present rate of adoptions, it would add more than a million people a year to the population of the United States—figures too frightening for any politician or ecologist to contemplate.

Yet, ironically, it is the world population explosion that may in the end offer hope to the frustrated adopters of the West. If the current predictions are accurate, there are parts of the world doomed to experience a crisis of such proportions that the release of a few babies for international adoption will hardly matter. The donor governments will give up their present objections to the practice; it is only the adopters' own governments, fearing large-scale immigration as they do, that are likely to create obstacles.

This prediction, too, has its flaws—it is by no means the most overpopulated countries at the moment that are the main participants in inter-country adoption. With children as with any other resource, international oversupply does not automatically alleviate local shortages.

The only societies we have studied that seem to combine ease of adoption, adequate care for all children, and a stable population are the homogeneous tribal societies that are vanishing so rapidly from the world. Why is it so difficult for us even to imagine the re-creation of such a society? The counter-culture with its tribes and communes has tried to create a situation in which children are raised by the group—but it is difficult to make such a group permanent enough to raise its own children, let alone to care for the children of others. One Marxist historian argues that capitalism has ejected man from this particular garden:

> The fact that communism preceded the emergence of classes in human history should not be taken to mean, in some Rousseauesque fashion, that man has lost a utopia ... Yet the glimpses into the quality of interpersonal relations that we are afforded from accounts of North American Indians and peoples in the rest of the world before they had experienced the alienation from the produce of their labour, and the divisiveness of being placed in fundamental competition with their fellow men ... do indeed make us somewhat envious. Behind the enormous variety of environmental adaptations and cultural embroideries which can be observed among these peoples, there did seem to be an underlying sense of self-respect and an ability to draw great satisfaction from work and personal relations. Perhaps most bitter to industrial man is the divisiveness which permeates relationships with those most dear, and the enmity between husbands and wives, parents and children.[4]

None the less, if most of us are honest with ourselves, we would be unwilling to trade the infinitely greater range of choices and possibilities of modern society for the vanished Utopia. And choice in personal relations is something we are constantly trying to expand, not to give up. Recent thinkers argue that today's sophisticated and complex societies have effectively replaced the family: that the withering of kin ties has come about simply because we no longer need them. We have other ways of supporting the old and the young, providing financial security, and controlling the individual ego in the service of the group.

We do have other ways of doing these things, but they do not always function very well. Nothing is more difficult than to compare them in this respect with other kinds of organization: were people happier, were children better cared for, in the tribal paradise? All we can say, finally, is that the system we have could work better than it does.

Is it possible to perfect these new mechanisms so that we no longer feel a sense of loss, justified or not, when we contemplate an organic society? Perhaps when adoption works as smoothly among us as it did among the Polynesians, we will know that we have arrived. Which of us, today, cares enough even about those closest to us to provide them with one of our children if that is what they lack? Which of us, indeed, would be willing to raise someone else's child if we were not motivated by our own childlessness? Even the last vestiges of the family system, the support of Granny or the taking-in of related children, are more easily found among the poor than among the privileged — and there are reasons for this embedded in the structure of our society.

> These child-caring functions the upper classes could delegate to their nannies. But the less affluent also have their proxy mothers, their nannas, although recruited by the ties of kinship rather than on the labour market, and relieving the mothers themselves for work rather than for leisure. Indeed, as incomes tend to become more equal and domestic help more scarce, it's these kin-based ties that have the edge here, both on the middle-class family that has to move around and on the upper-class family that can no longer get servants.[5]

It is worth noting that in groups and nations that have practised widespread adoption, those who care for children do not do it on their own. Family, friends, and society itself share the responsibility in tangible ways. Far from being irresponsible, it may be that mothers who agitate for day care, neighbourhood centres, nursery schools, and role-sharing in the home are trying to enable themselves to be more responsible parents. The loneliness of the mother and small child in today's big cities may be unprecedented; it is certain that it makes motherhood more difficult. Easy adoption, and widespread care for children in general, can only be helped by efforts to re-integrate parents into society.

Finally, the lesson to be learned by seeing how others have practised adoption is that a fundamental re-examination of our own practice is not to be feared, but welcomed. There is much that is good about it, and much that could be changed. Prejudice against other ways of doing things can only narrow the range of possibilities open to us, to the detriment of our own children.

Abbreviations used in the text

A.B.A.A. Association of British Adoption Agencies
A.F.D.C. Aid to Families with Dependent Children
AID Agency for International Development
A.R.E. Adoption Resource Exchange
ARENA Adoption Resource Exchange of North America
C.W.L.A. Child Welfare League of America
D.H.S.S. Department of Health and Social Security
4th N.A.C.A.C. 4th North American Conference on Adoptable
  Children
I.S.S. International Social Service
I.U.C.W. International Union for Child Welfare

Notes

1 INTRODUCTION

1 John Bowlby, *Child Care and the Growth of Love* (Penguin Books, Harmondsworth, 1953).
2 Dr Mia Kellmer Pringle in *The Times* (London, October 16th, 1973).
3 'Adoption in Perspective: Vision and Reality', Proceedings of the 4th North American Conference on Adoptable Children, Washington, D.C., (March 14th–17th, 1974).
4 Joseph Reid at 4th N.A.C.A.C.
5 Jean Seglow, Mia Kellmer Pringle, and Peter Wedge, *Growing Up Adopted* (National Foundation for Educational Research in England and Wales, 1972).

2 THE EXTENDED FAMILY

1 G. R. Driver and J. C. Miles, *The Babylonian Laws* (Oxford University Press, London, 1955), vol. II, *Laws of Hammu-Rabi*.
2 Ibid., vol. I, *Legal Commentary* (1952).
3 G. R. Driver and J. C. Miles, *The Assyrian Laws* (Oxford University Press, London, 1935).
4 *Encyclopedia Judaica*, entry on Adoption.
5 Ibid.
6 Clarke Hall and Morrison, *The Law Relating to Children* (Butterworth, London, 1972).
7 Edward Gibbon, *The Decline and Fall of the Roman Empire* (Harrap, London, 1949), p. 131.
8 W. W. Buckland, *A Text-Book of Roman Law* (Cambridge University Press, London, 3rd edition, revised by Peter Stein, 1963).
9 Ibid.
10 Ibid.

11 Emily Ahern, *The Cult of the Dead in a Chinese Village* (Stanford University Press, 1973).
12 Ibid.
13 Claude Lévi-Strauss, *The Elementary Structures of Kinship* (Eyre & Spottiswoode, London, new edition, 1969).
14 *Mayne's Treatise on Hindu Law and Usage* (Higginbothams Ltd., Madras, 11th edition, ed. N. Chandrasekhara Aiyar, 1953).
15 Marc Bloch, *Feudal Society* (Routledge & Kegan Paul Ltd., London, 1962), vol. II.
16 F. L. Ganshof, *Feudalism* (Longman, London, 1961).
17 Philippe Aries, *Centuries of Childhood* (Penguin Books, Harmondsworth, 1973).
18 Jack Goody, 'Adoption in Cross-Cultural Perspective', *Comparative Studies in Society and History*, vol. II, no. 1 (January, 1969).
19 A. R. Radcliffe-Brown, *Structure and Function in Primitive Society* (Cohen & West Ltd., London, 1969).
20 E. E. Evans-Pritchard, *The Position of Women in Primitive Societies* (Faber & Faber, London, 1965).
21 A. R. Radcliffe-Brown and Daryll Forde, *African Systems of Kinship and Marriage* (Oxford University Press, London, 1950).
22 Mervyn Jones in *The New Statesman*, April 12th, 1974.
23 Radcliffe-Brown and Forde, op. cit.
24 *International Encyclopedia of the Social Sciences*, entry on Adoption.
25 Esther Goody, *Contexts of Kinship* (Cambridge University Press, London, 1973).
26 Lévi-Strauss, op. cit.
27 Ibid.
28 Robert Briffault, *The Mothers* (Allen & Unwin Ltd., London, 1927).
29 Esther Goody, op. cit.
30 Lucy P. Mair, *An African People in the Twentieth Century* (Routledge & Sons Ltd., London, 1934).
31 Robert Levy, 'Tahitian Adoption as a Psychological Message', in Vern Carroll, ed., *Adoption in Eastern Oceania* (University of Hawaii Press, Honolulu, 1970).
32 Kenelm Burridge, *Tangu Traditions* (Oxford University Press, London, 1969).
33 Jack Goody, op. cit.

3 THE REBIRTH OF ADOPTION

1 Philippe Aries, *Centuries of Childhood*, op. cit.
2 Ibid.

3 Jack Goody, *Comparative Studies in Kinship* (Routledge & Kegan Paul Ltd, London, 1969).

4 Ivy Pinchbeck and Margaret Hewitt, *Children in English Society* (Routledge & Kegan Paul Ltd, London, 1969), vol. I.

5 Nigel Middleton, *When Family Failed* (Victor Gollancz, London, 1971).

6 Ibid.

7 Ibid.

8 Ibid.

9 Ibid.

10 The Countess of Roussillon in *All's Well That Ends Well*, I, iii, 150–6.

11 Marie-Dora Gressier, 'L'Adoption' (Cridon-Ouest, May 1971).

12 Theodore Zeldin, *France 1848–1945* (The Clarendon Press, Oxford, 1973), vol. I.

13 Gressier, op. cit.

14 Arthur W. Calhoun, *A Social History of the American Family* (Barnes & Noble, New York, 1917), vol. I.

15 Ibid., vol. II.

16 '*Homes for the Homeless*' (Children's Home Society of New Jersey, September, 1970), vol. LXXVIII, no. I.

17 Ibid.

18 Rael Jean Isaac, *Adopting a Child Today* (Harper & Row, New York, 1965).

19 Edmund Leach, *Genesis as Myth* (Jonathan Cape, London, 1969).

20 Middleton, op. cit.

21 Ibid.

22 *Hansard*, 1926, v. 191 p. 243.

23 *Hansard*, 1926, v. 192 p. 931.

24 Ibid., loc. cit.

25 Ibid., loc. cit.

26 Ibid., loc. cit.

27 Ibid., loc. cit.

28 Ibid., loc. cit.

29 Middleton, op. cit.

4 THE WEST TODAY

1 I.U.C.W., Open Letter no. 15.

2 George Armstrong in *The Guardian*, December 11th, 1973.

3 Dr Giuseppe Cicorella, President, Comité International d'Entente des Associations de Foyers Adoptifs. Private communication, March 4th, 1974.

4 *France-Soir*, December 19th, 1973.
5 *Le Monde*, December 14th, 1973.
6 'Policies, Programmes and Laws for the Protection of Children
   for Adoption and Foster Placement in Israel' (Israeli Government publication, October 1973).
7 Interview with the author, May 20th, 1974.
8 Joseph Goldstein, Anna Freud and Albert J. Solnit, *Beyond the
   Best Interests of the Child* (The Free Press, New York, 1973).
9 *The Sunday Times* (London), May 19th, 1974.
10 Jane Rowe and Lydia Lambert, *Children Who Wait* (Association
   of British Adoption Agencies, 1973).
11 Ibid.
12 Ibid.
13 Bowlby, *Child Care and the Growth of Love*, op. cit.
14 Proceedings of 4th N.A.C.A.C.
15 Ibid.
16 Ibid.
17 Ibid.

5 EASTERN CONTRASTS

1 Adoption Ordinance 1942 (as amended); *Laws of Sarawak 1958*,
   Ch. 91.
2 Adoption of Children Proclamation 1952.
3 H. Kent Geiger, *The Family in Soviet Russia* (Harvard University
   Press, Cambridge, Mass., 1968).
4 Bertolt Brecht, *Parables For The Theatre* (Penguin Books,
   Harmondsworth, new edition, 1966) (first published 1949).
5 Geiger, op. cit.
6 Ibid.
7 Quoted in *Survey*, Summer 1973.
8 Urie Bronfenbrenner, *Two Worlds of Childhood* (Penguin Books,
   Harmondsworth, 1974).
9 Ibid.
10 *Survey*, July 1963.
11 Martin C. Yang, *A Chinese Village* (Kegan Paul, London, 1948).
12 Olga Lang, *Chinese Family and Society* (Yale University Press,
   New Haven, 1946).
13 Marion Levy, *The Family Revolution in Modern China* (Oxford
   University Press, London, 1949).
14 K. S. Karol, *China: The Other Communism*, tr. T. Baistow
   (Heinemann, London, 1967).
15 Ibid.

16 Robert O. Blood, *The Family* (The Free Press, New York, 1972).
17 William J. Goode, *The Family* (Prentice-Hall, New Jersey, 1964).
18 *International Encyclopedia of the Social Sciences*, entry on Adoption.
19 Japan *Times*, January 4th, 1974.
20 Ibid.
21 Gunnar Myrdal, *Asian Drama* (Allen Lane: The Penguin Press, London, 1968).
22 I.U.C.W., Open Letter, no. 17.
23 *The Observer*, December 16th, 1973.
24 *The Sunday Times* (London), February 24th, 1974.

6 INTER-COUNTY ADOPTION

1 Many of the social workers I interviewed did not wish their names to be used.
2 André Gunder Frank, *Capitalism and Underdevelopment in Latin America* (Penguin Books, Harmondsworth, 1971).
3 John E. Adams and Hyung Bok Kim, 'A Fresh Look at Inter-country Adoptions', *Children*, vol. 18, no. 6 (Nov–Dec 1971).
4 Helen Miller, 'Korea's International Children', *Lutheran Social Welfare*, vol. II, no. 2 (Summer 1971).
5 Adams and Kim, op. cit.
6 'Child Welfare in Vietnam Fact Sheet', AID, January 31st, 1974.
7 Dr James R. Dumpson's testimony before Senate Committee on the Judiciary, 'Relief and Rehabilitation of War Victims in Indochina', May 11th, 1973 (U.S. Govt. Printing Office).
8 Adams and Kim, op. cit.
9 Dumpson, in 'Relief and rehabilitation', op. cit.
10 Ibid.
11 Ibid.
12 *Melbourne Age*, August 16th, 1973.
13 Myrdal, *Asian Drama*, op. cit.
14 Dumpson, in 'Relief and Rehabilitation', op. cit.
15 Pyongyang *Times*, quoted in *The Guardian*, June 20th, 1973.
16 Dr John M. Levinson, in 'Relief and Rehabilitation', op. cit.
17 Proceedings of 4th N.A.C.A.C.
18 Private communication, April 4th, 1974.
19 Proceedings of 4th N.A.C.A.C.
20 Ibid.
21 John Adams at 4th N.A.C.A.C.

1 David Fanshel, *Far From the Reservation* (The Scarecrow Press, Inc., Metuchen, N.J., 1972).
2 *New York Times*, special report, 1971.
3 Bernice Q. Madison and Michael Schapiro, 'Black Adoption — Issues and Policies: Review of the Literature', *The Social Service Review*, vol. 47, no. 4 (December 1973).
4 'Homes for the Homeless', *Children's Home Society of New Jersey*, September, 1970.
5 Madison & Schapiro, op. cit.
6 *The New Yorker* Report on the 1970 census, October 22nd, 1973.
7 Ibid.
8 Proceedings of the New Orleans Black Child Advocacy Adoption Conference, 1972 (B.C.D.I.).
9 Proceedings of the Boston Black Child Care Advocacy Conference, 1973 (B.C.D.I.).
10 Proceedings of the Memphis Black Child Advocacy Adoption Conference (B.C.D.I.).
11 Ibid.
12 Elizabeth Herzog, Cecelia E. Sudia, and Jane Harwood, 'Finding Families for Black Children', in *Children*, vol. 18, no. 4 (July–August 1971).
13 'Homes for the Homeless', *Children's Home Society of New Jersey*, September 1970.
14 Elizabeth A. Lawder, *et al.*, 'A Study of Black Adoption Families: A Comparison of a Traditional and a Quasi-Adoption Program', C.W.L.A., 1971.
15 Ibid.
16 Ibid.
17 Edward T. Weaver, 'Subsidized Adoption: A Report to the Illinois General Assembly', April 1st, 1970.
18 Trudy Bradley Festinger, *An Exploration of Caseworkers' Perceptions of Adoptive Applicants*, C.W.L.A., 1967.
19 Trudy Bradley Festinger, 'Why Some Choose Not to Adopt through Agencies', Metropolitan Applied Research Center, Inc., 1972.
20 Proceedings of the Boston Black Child Care Advocacy Conference.
21 Interview with the author, March 1974.
22 Dawn Day Wachtel, 'Adoption Agencies and the Adoption of Black Children: Social Change and Equal Opportunity in Adoption'. Unpublished Ph.D. dissertation, University of Michigan, 1972.

23 Florence Kreech, 'Adoption Outreach', *Child Welfare*, vol. LII, no. 10 (December 1973).
24 'Meeting on Placement and Adoption of Vietnamese Children in American Homes', AID, July 25th–26th, 1973.
25 Interview with the author, March 1974.
26 Interview with the author, March 1974.
27 Kai T. Erikson, ed., *In Search of Common Ground: Conversations with Erik H. Erikson and Huey P. Newton* (W. W. Norton Inc., New York, 1973).
28 *The Guardian*, February 16th, 1973.
29 *Nova*, December 1972.
30 *The Sunday Times* (London), February 17th, 1974.
31 *The Guardian*, September 26th, 1973.

8 THE ADOPTERS

1 Blood, *The Family*.
2 Michael Humphrey, *The Hostage Seekers* (National Bureau for Co-operation in Child Care, 1969).
3 Myrdal, *Asian Drama*.
4 P. W. Toussieng, summarized in M. L. Kellmer Pringle, *Adoption—Facts and Fallacies* (National Bureau for Co-operation in Child Care, 1966).
5 H. David Kirk, *Shared Fate* (The Free Press, New York, 1964).

9 THE NATURAL PARENTS

1 Lois Raynor, *Giving Up a Baby for Adoption* (A.B.A.A., 1971).
2 Michael Bohman, *Adopted Children and Their Families* (Proprius, Stockholm, 1970).
3 Jean Seglow, Mia Kellmer Pringle and Peter Wedge, *Growing Up Adopted*, op. cit.
4 Leontine Young, *Out of Wedlock* (McGraw-Hill, New York, 1954).
5 Interview in *The Guardian*, March 28th 1974.
6 Raynor, op. cit.
7 Memorandum of the U.S. Department of Health, Education and Welfare, August 2nd, 1972.

10 THE ADOPTEES

1 Jack Goody, *The Character of Kinship* (Cambridge University Press, London, 1973.)

2   Mary D. Salter Ainsworth, *et al.*, 'Infant-Mother Attachment and Social Development: "Socialisation" as a Product of Reciprocal Responsiveness to Signals' in Martin P.M. Richards, ed., *The Integration of a Child into a Social World* (Cambridge University Press, London, 1974).

3   Bowlby, *Child Care and the Growth of Love*, op. cit.

4   Ibid.

5   Alfred Kadushin, 'Reversibility of Trauma: A Follow-Up Study of Children Adopted When Older', *Social Work*, October 1967.

6   Ibid.

7   *Boston Globe*, May 28th, 1974.

8   John Triseliotis, *In Search of Origins* (Routledge & Kegan Paul Ltd., London, 1973).

9   Benson Jaffee, 'Adoption Outcome: A Two-Generation View', *Child Welfare*, vol. LIII, no. 4 (April 1974).

10 John Bowlby, *Attachment and Loss* (Hogarth Press, London, 1973), vol. II, *Separation*.

11 *The Times*, November 12th, 1973.

12 Bowlby, op. cit.

11   GENETICS

1   Helene Deutsch, *The Psychology of Women: A Psychoanalytic Interpretation* (Grune & Stratton, New York, 1945).

2   Bowlby, *Attachment and Loss*, op. cit.

3   Harold M. Skeels, 'Effects of Adoption on Children from Institutions', *Children*, vol 12, no. 1 (Jan–Feb 1965).

4   Ibid.

5   Christopher Jencks, *et al.*, *Inequality* (Allen Lane, London, 1973).

6   Arthur R. Jensen, *Genetics and Education* (Methuen & Co., London, 1972.)

7   Jencks, *et al.*, op. cit.

8   M. L. Kellmer Pringle, *Deprivation and Education* (Longmans, London, 1965).

9   Bruno Bettelheim, *The Informed Heart* (Thames & Hudson, London, 1961).

12   THE GO-BETWEENS

1   C.W.L.A. Newsletter, vol. 3, no. 1 (Spring 1973).

2   Wachtel, 'Adoption Agencies and the Adoption of Black Children', op. cit.

3 'Homes for the Homeless', op. cit.
4 *The Times*, January 5th, 1968.
5 Bradley, op. cit.
6 Wachtel, op. cit.
7 Esther Glickman, *Child Placement through Clinically Oriented Casework* (Columbia University Press, 1957).
8 Carl and Helen Doss, *If You Adopt a Child* (Holt, New York, 1957).
9 Louise B. Dillow, 'The Group Process in Adoptive Home-finding', *Children*, vol. 15, no. 4, (July–August, 1968).
10 Edith M. Chappelear and Joyce E. Fried, 'Helping Adopting Couples Come to Grips with Their New Parental Roles', *Children*, vol. 14, no. 6 (November–December 1967).
11 *New York Times*, February 20th 1973.
12 Ibid.
13 *New York Times*, April 27th, 1974.

13 CONCLUSION: THE BABY FAMINE

1 Donald W. Winnicott, 'Adopted Children in Adolescence', in *Social Work in Adoption: Collected Papers*, edited by Robert Tod (Longman, London, 1971).
2 Television programme on B.B.C. 2, Autumn 1973.
3 Dr S. L. Henderson Smith in *Pulse*, February 23rd, 1974.
4 Eleanor Burke Leacock's Introduction to Frederick Engels' *The Origin of the Family, Private Property and the State* (Lawrence & Wishart, London, 1972).
5 Goody, *Comparative Studies in Kinship*, op. cit.

Select Bibliography

Vern Carroll, ed., *Adoption in Eastern Oceania* (University of Hawaii Press, 1970).
> This shows more clearly than any other single book the vast differences in different cultures' ideas of adoption.

Joseph Goldstein, Anna Freud, and Albert J. Solnit, *Beyond the Best Interests of the Child* (The Free Press, New York, 1973).
> Proposals for radical change in adoption legislation, likely to be very influential.

H. David Kirk, *Shared Fate* (The Free Press, New York, 1964).
> A perceptive account of the psychological aspects of adoption.

Margaret Kornitzer, *Adoption* (Putnam & Co., London, 1970).
> A useful primer for people thinking about adopting.

Jane Rowe, *Parents, Children and Adoption* (Routledge & Kegan Paul Ltd., London, 1966).
> A handbook for social workers, but interesting reading for adoptive parents as well.

Jane Rowe and Lydia Lambert, *Children Who Wait* (Association of British Adoption Agencies, London, 1973).
> This book shows why there are still children in care in spite of the baby shortage.

Jean Seglow, Mia Kellmer Pringle and Peter Wedge, *Growing Up Adopted* (National Foundation for Educational Research, London, 1972).
> The report of the National Child Development Study: an incomparable source of facts about adoption.

Index

237